A Touch of Wonder

A Touch of Wonder

STAYING
IN LOVE
WITH LIFE

Arthur Gordon

Fleming H. Revell
A Division of Baker Book House Co
Grand Rapids, Michigan 49516

© 1974 by Arthur Gordon

Published by Fleming H. Revell
a division of Baker Book House Company
P.O. Box 6287, Grand Rapids, MI 49516-6287

New paperback edition published 1996

Third printing, March 1998

Printed in the United States of America

ISBN 0-8007-5602-9

"On the Dunes" is taken from *Collected Poems* by Sara Teasdale and is reprinted
with permission of Macmillan Publishing Company. Copyright 1920 by
Macmillan Publishing Company, renewed 1948 by Mamie T. Wheless.

The following are reprinted with permission of *Woman's Day Magazine*, a Fawcett
publication: "Beautiful Dreamer," "How Wonderful You Are," "The Search,"
"Act as If," "The Deadly Art of Nonliving," "Freedom Is a Two-edged Sword,"
and "Welcome to Danger."

Grateful appreciation is expressed to *Reader's Digest* of Pleasantville, New York,
for permission to use the articles in this volume that appeared previously in that
publication.

"The Miraculous Staircase," December 1966; "Enthusiasm," December 1958; "Be
Bold," May 1956 are reprinted with permission of *Guideposts Magazine.*
Copyright by Guideposts Associates, Inc., Carmel, New York.

"The End of the Journey" is published with the permission of the Reader's
Digest, Inc.

For current information about all releases from Baker Book House, visit our
web site:

http://www.bakerbooks.com

For Pam
who was there

Contents

Prayer of a Writer

Lord of all things, whose wondrous gifts to man
Include the shining symbols known as words,
Grant that I may use their mighty power
Only for good. Help me to pass on
Small fragments of Your wisdom, truth, and love.
Teach me to touch the unseen, lonely heart
With laughter, or the quick release of tears.
Let me portray the courage that endures
Defiant in the face of pain or death;
The kindness and the gentleness of those
Who fight against the anger of the world;
The beauty hidden in the smallest things;
The mystery, the wonder of it all . . . .
Open my ears, my eyes; unlock my heart.
Speak through me, Lord, if it be Your will. *Amen.*

Introduction

What should an introduction introduce—a book or the writer behind the book? Perhaps it doesn't matter, so long as it's done quickly.

This book? Well, it's not autobiography; that would require stern self-honesty, whereas here I appear with my best foot resolutely forward. It's not really a self-help manual either—no surefire formula for success, no easy blueprint for peace of mind.

No, it's just a book that reflects one man's way of looking at things. Simple things, mostly. Things that happen to all of us sooner or later. And the underlying theme is also quite simple: It's that almost always there's a lot more to these commonplace happenings than meets the casual eye—and that most people would find a lot more in them if only they would pause and look and feel and care just a bit more than they do.

It's also a book that conveys, I hope, one man's sense of gratitude for the endless free gifts that life offers—and his conviction that in some inexplicable way those who appreciate life the most are given the most to appreciate. As some sage once observed, "It's the person who likes to pat dogs to whom dogs come for pats." Exactly so.

As for the person behind the book, who can really answer the question, "Who are you?" I'm an editor-turned-writer with a good many typewriter-miles behind me now—years filled with work, play, friends, children, dogs, cats (and a couple of raccoons), successes, failures, challenges, and a few small disasters. Not an extraordinary life, by any means. But luckier than most, I think. And happier than most, I know. It's a life that has followed the classic pattern of running away from the ancestral past and then returning to it when you begin to be an ancestor yourself. A life strangely drawn—as you will see in many of the pages that follow—to the lonely beaches and tawny marshes of the Georgia coast where I first became aware that in good times or bad, life is a marvelous succession of wonders.

Please don't look in these pages for firm organization or neat chronology. A book of this kind can be read backward or forward or even sideways. You can start at the beginning or at the end.

Wherever you start, I hope you will accept it for what it's meant to be: an invitation to fall in love with life—and thereby set in motion the mysterious dynamics that will cause life to love you right back.

ARTHUR GORDON

A Touch of Wonder

1

The Gift of Caring

Most of us spend our lives trying to escape from self-centeredness. Maybe that's the whole point, the whole challenge, what the whole thing is all about. Some of us succeed better than others. It seems to me that the ones who have most success are those who somehow turn self-caring into what might be called other-caring.

It takes courage to be an other-carer, because people who care run the risk of being hurt. It's not easy to let your guard down, open your heart, react with sympathy or compassion or indignation or enthusiasm when usually it's much easier—and sometimes much safer—not to get involved.

But people who take the risk make a tremendous discovery: The more things you care about, and the more intensely you care, the more alive you are.

This capacity for caring can illuminate any relationship: marriage, family, friendships—even the ties of affection that often join humans and animals. Each of us is born with some of it, but whether we let it expand or diminish is largely up to us.

To care, you have to surrender the armor of indifference. You have to be willing to act, to make the first move. Once at sunset my small daughter and I were watching the tide come in. It was a quiet evening, calm and opalescent. The waves sent thin sheets of molten gold across the dry sand—closer and closer. Finally, almost like a caress, an arm of the ocean curled around the base of the dune. And my daughter said, pensively, "Isn't it wonderful—how much the sea cares about the land?"

She was right, with the infallible instinct of childhood: It *was* a kind of caring. The land was merely passive—and so it waited. But the sea cared—and so it came. The lesson was all there in that lovely symbol: the willingness to act, to approach, to be absorbed, and in the absorption—to be fulfilled.

Wedding by the Sea

From the start, they didn't want a formal wedding. No bridesmaids, no wedding march, nothing like that. "The old language and the old ritual are beautiful," our daughter said, "but they belong to millions of people. Ken and I want something of our own."

In an old town like ours, tradition binds with silver chains. "Well," we said a bit doubtfully, "it's your wedding. How do you want it, and when, and where?"

"At sundown," said Dana dreamily, shaking back her long blond hair. "On the beach. As near the ocean as we can get. With a minister who understands how we feel and who can say some words that belong in the twentieth century."

"But what will you *wear?*" her mother asked, naturally.

"A long white dress," she said. "With a bouquet made of sea oats. But no shoes. I want to feel the sand under my feet. I don't know why—but I do."

She's choosing the beach, I said to myself, *because you taught her to love it. Some deep instinct in her knows that life makes tremendous silent statements where sand and salt water meet. She's following that instinct, and she's right.*

So I was pleased, but still a faint, strange sense of apprehension seemed to shadow the pleasure. Nothing to do with Ken—a fine boy, strong and tall, with a skilled surfer's easy grace and a teaching career stretching out ahead of him. Nothing to do with anything graspable, really. *You're afraid,* I told myself finally, *that's it. Afraid that something very*

important in your life may be ending. Afraid that a closeness may be
vanishing. You may be able to conceal the feeling, or even deny it,
but you won't be able to push it away. It goes too deep for reason—or
for words.

"Arrange for a big high tide, will you?" said Dana, giving
us both a casual hug. "And no thunderstorms, please."

"I'm not entirely in charge of such things," I told her.
"But we'll do the best we can."

The time came. We stood—friends, neighbors,
relatives—in a little amphitheatre made by the dunes. Behind us the dying sun hurled spears of amber light. Ahead,
the ocean came surging joyously, all ivory and jade and
gold. The young minister stood facing us, the crimson-
lined hood of his robe fluttering in the wind, tongues of
foam licking at his heels. He had to lift his voice above the
clamor of the waves.

> Friends, we are here this afternoon to share with Ken and
> Dana a most important moment in their lives. In places like
> this they have learned to know and love each other. Now they
> have decided to live their lives together as husband and
> wife . . . .

In places like this . . . . Under the overlay of time, I
could feel the pictures form and dissolve in my mind. Years
ago on this same beach, not many yards away, a placid pool
left by the ebbing tide. One moment a three-year-old playing at the edge. The next moment—incredibly—vanished.
And the heart-stopping realization, the frantic plunge, the
lunge that raised the small dripping figure back into the
sunlight, the overwhelming relief that somehow she had
remembered what she had been taught about holding her
breath. Then the wide gray eyes opening and the small,

reproachful voice: "Why didn't you come *sooner?* It's all dark and bubbly down there!"

Or the day years later, when she was perhaps eleven or twelve, and we found the old pelican, sick and shivering. Nothing could be done; we had to watch him die. And the impact as death for the first time became a reality, and the piercing pain of compassion striking the unarmored spirit. "Oh," she said finally through her tears, groping for something to ease her anguish, "I'm glad we didn't know him very well."

And then, still later, the golden afternoons when she would go out saying gravely that she had to walk her dog, but knowing that we knew she really hoped to find Ken surfing. He was hardly aware of her then, but she would sit on a dune with arms clasped around her knees and her heart full of love and longing and the big German shepherd motionless as a statue by her side.

In places like this . . . . Why does time slide by so fast, I asked myself. *Why does nothing stay?*

Serenely the young minister's voice went on:

> We have been invited to hear Ken and Dana as they promise to face the future together, accepting whatever joy or sadness may lie ahead. These surroundings were not chosen by chance. Those who love the sea can hear in it the heartbeat of Creation as the tides ebb and flow, the sun rises and sets, and the stars come nightly to the sky. For the beauty around us, for the strength it offers, for the peace it brings, we are grateful.

Yes, I thought, *it does give strength. To find endurance all we have to do is seek out places where great and elemental things prevail. For some of us the sea. For some the mountains, as the psalmist knew. I will lift up mine eyes . . . .*

Now the words were being spoken directly to the young couple:

Dana and Ken, nothing is easier than saying words.
Nothing is harder than living them, day after day.
What you promise today must be renewed and redecided tomorrow and each day that stretches out before you.
At the end of this ceremony, legally you will be man and wife, but still you must decide each day that you want to be married.

Can they understand that? I asked myself, watching the clear young profiles. *Can they possibly grasp it now? or will the realization take years, as it has for most of us, and then come so quietly that they're not even sure that it's there?*
The young minister was saying tenderly:

All of us know that you are deeply in love. But beyond the warmth and glow, the excitement and romance, what is love, really?
Real love is caring as much about the welfare and happiness of your marriage partner as about your own.
Real love is not possessive or jealous; it is liberating; it sets you free to become your best self.
Real love is not total absorption in each other; it is looking outward in the same direction—together.
Love makes burdens lighter, because you divide them. It makes joys more intense, because you share them. It makes you stronger, so that you can reach out and become involved with life in ways you dared not risk alone.

True, I was thinking. *All true. But you can't learn it from hearing it. You have to learn it by living it, and even then no one but a saint can apply more than fragments of it to his own marriage or his own life. All we can do, even the best of us, is try. And even the trying is hard.*

Now the time had come for the questions, and indeed the language did belong to the twentieth century:

> Ken, will you take Dana to be your wife? Will you love and respect her? Will you be honest with her always? Will you stand by her through whatever may come? Will you make whatever adjustments are necessary so that you can genuinely share your life with her?

"I will," said the tall boy, and to the same questions the slender girl gave the same answer.

Now the minister's steady gaze fell upon us.

> Who brings this woman to stand beside this man?

"We do," my wife and I said together. We could not give our child away, for she was not our possession. She was uniquely and eternally herself. And yet, but for our own love, she would not be here under this tranquil sky, close to this restless sea.

The same question to Ken's parents. The same answer. And then a challenge to the four of us:

> Are you willing, now and always, to support and strengthen this marriage by upholding both Ken and Dana with your love and concern?

"We are," we said, and now all of us were a part of the commitment. No favoritism. No side-taking. Just a quiet, constant defense against the fierce centrifugal forces that threaten every marriage. *This at least,* I thought, *is wholly within our power; this much we can do.*

Now for a moment the wind seemed to hush itself and around us the swaying sea oats grew almost still. I saw Dana's fingers tremble as she put her hand in Ken's, waiting for the ancient symbol of fidelity and love.

"I give you this ring," the tall boy said. "Wear it with love and joy. I choose you to be my wife this day and every day."

"I accept this ring," our child said in a small voice—but a woman's voice. "I will wear it with love and joy. I choose you to be my husband this day and every day."

Silence, then, for a moment or two. No one stirred. The faces of the onlookers were touched with something indefinable, a kind of timelessness, a sense of life fulfilling itself and moving on. *Perhaps this is the way that everything of consequence begins,* I thought. *No certainty. No guarantees. Just a choice, an intention, a promise, a hope. . . .*

The minister reached forward and took the couple's clasped hands in his own.

> Ken and Dana, we have heard you promise to share your lives in marriage. We recognize and respect the covenant you have made. It's not a minister standing before you that makes your marriage real, but the honesty and sincerity of what you have said and done here before your friends and parents and in the sight of God. On behalf of all those present, I take your hands and acknowledge that you are husband and wife.

He smiled and released their hands.

> Now the ceremony is over and the experience of living day by day as married people is about to begin. Go forth to meet it gladly. Love life, so that life will love you. The blessing of God be with you. So be it.

So be it, I thought, watching Dana kiss her husband and turn to embrace her mother. *So be it!* cried all the hugs and the handshakes, the excited laughter and the unashamed tears. *So be it,* murmured the wind and the waves, turning away once more from human things.

And when I looked for the apprehension that had been in me, it was gone.

Fraidy Cat

We got her at the place for friendless or abandoned animals—a tiny gray-and-white kitten whose eyes were still blue. Just an alley cat, nameless, homeless, too young to lap milk from a saucer—we had to feed her with an eyedropper. She didn't like the strange new world in which she found herself. She hid under the bed and cried. We laughed and called her Fraidy Cat.

She soon got used to us, of course. She slept a lot and played games with balls of wadded paper. I never saw her chase her tail, as kittens are supposed to do. But she had a good time.

She had an even better time when we moved to the country. She was half-grown, then, and liked to stalk things in the tall grass behind the house. Twice she brought home a mouse for us to admire, and once—a bird. Fortunately the bird wasn't hurt, so we took it away from her and let it go. She seemed to think our distinction between mice and birds was pretty silly. Logically, she was right.

She was an aloof little beast in those days—I say "little" because she remained a very small cat. She didn't show much affection for anyone. In fact, if you tried to pet her when she wasn't in the mood, she would dig her claws in harder than was pleasant—or even bite. This didn't bother me, of course, because I am really a dog man. I can take cats or leave them alone.

We acquired a dog soon after we moved to the country, a

friendly boxer named Major. Fraidy loathed him. For the first month or so, if he came too close, she would spit and rake his nose, leaving him hurt and bewildered. I was rather indignant about this—after all, I'm a dog man—and I slapped Fraidy once or twice for assaulting Major. "Who do you think you are?" I asked her. "Try to remember you're nothing but a cat!"

While she was still too young, in our opinion, for such goings-on, Fraidy decided to become a mother. When the time came, however, she didn't hide away like most cats; she stuck close to us. Maybe she had a hunch it was going to be tough. It was. There was only a single kitten, much too big. She couldn't handle it herself; I had to help her. It took all my strength, and I thought she would bite me, but she didn't. She just watched me, her yellow eyes glassy with pain. Afterwards, she licked my hand. But the kitten was born dead.

"Never mind, Fraidy," we said. "You'll have better luck next time."

For days she was gaunt and thin; she looked for the kitten everywhere. I believe she thought Major was responsible for its disappearance—all her old distrust of him came back, for a while. She got over that, but one thing she did not get over: her gratitude to me. She followed me from room to room, and if I sat down she would jump into my lap, put her forefeet on my chest, and stare into my face with the most soulful look imaginable.

"Typical woman," my wife said, laughing. "In love with her obstetrician."

"It's just misplaced maternal instinct," I said. "She'll get over it as soon as she has some kittens."

Nature, it seemed, had the same idea, because before very long Fraidy was pregnant again. We figured she would have at least two kittens, this time. Smaller ones. We were very happy for her. She seemed sleepy and satisfied.

Then one day, not long ago, she developed a cough. We thought nothing of it; her appetite was good. She seemed somewhat lethargic, but after all, her time was almost due. Then, early yesterday morning, she came up from the kitchen where she slept and jumped on our bed. She curled up in my lap and looked at me. She meowed unhappily. "What's the matter with this fool cat?" I said. "What's she trying to tell us?"

All yesterday she didn't eat. She even refused water. In the evening, finally, I called a vet. There are good vets, I guess, and bad ones. This one—when he saw her—said it seemed to be just a cold. No fever. Nothing very wrong. That was yesterday.

This morning Fraidy Cat dragged herself upstairs again, but this time she couldn't jump onto the bed. She was too weak. The roof of her mouth was very pale; her eyes were glazed.

I telephoned another vet. It was Sunday morning, and early, but he said to bring her over. I did. He examined her carefully. He knew his business; you can always tell. "I'm sorry," he said. "Uterine infection. I'm afraid the kittens are dead."

"Can't you operate?" I said. "Can't you save her?"

He shook his head. "I could try. But it would just prolong things. She's pretty far gone now." He looked at my face. He was a kind man and he loved animals. "I'd put her away," he said gently, "if I were you."

After a while I nodded my head.

"Now?" said the vet, "or after you've gone?"

"I'll stay with her," I said.

He brought the hypodermic needle and the nembutal.

"It doesn't hurt," he said. "She'll go to sleep, that's all." The needle went home, quick and merciful.

She was just an ordinary alley cat. She had no pedigree, no clever tricks. But I remembered how she'd roll over on the path when we'd drive up in the car. I remembered how she loved to eat slivers of melon from our breakfast plates. I remembered how she liked to have her ears scratched, and how she licked my hand the day I had to hurt her so terribly, the day her kitten was born dead.

I stood there with my hand touching her so that perhaps she would not be afraid. "It's all right, Fraidy," I said. "Go to sleep. Go to sleep." And at last she put her head down on her clean little paws and closed her eyes.

I felt blindly for my pocketbook. It wasn't there. "I haven't any money," I said. "I'll have to send it to you."

"That's all right," the vet said. "Don't bother."

I touched her ear for the last time and turned back to the door. It was a golden summer morning, calm, serene. Down in the meadow a gigantic willow tree made a burst of greenness against the sky.

I got in the car quickly and drove away. But not far down the road I stopped the car and put my forehead against the steering wheel and wept. Because she was such a little cat. Because she had tried to tell me that she was sick, that she was in trouble, and I hadn't helped her. Not until too late. And I felt the awful emptiness that comes from not knowing how much you love something until you have lost it.

The Quiet Power of Compassion

Not long ago I attended a memorial service for a well-known business leader. In a subdued atmosphere of mourning, various friends paid tribute to him. Near the end, a young black man arose. The other speakers had been assured and eloquent, but this one, under great emotional stress, could barely speak at all. A deep hush fell as he struggled for words.

Finally, with tears streaming down his face, he told the gathering that when he was just an office boy, the industrialist had noticed him, helped him, encouraged him, paid for his education. "For a long time," the young man said, "I was no good to him or anyone else. I just failed and kept on failing. But he never gave up on me—and he never let me give up on myself."

He went on to say that anyone could support a success, but that only a rare and wonderful person could continue to have faith in a failure. Now that person was gone, and he had lost his best friend. When at last his voice faltered to a halt and he sat down, people everywhere were weeping, not just for the leader who was gone but for the sorrow of the follower who had revealed so much of himself. When the service ended, I had the strange conviction that somehow all of us had been changed for the better, that a tiny part of each one of us would never be the same again.

Later I spoke of this to a friend, a psychiatrist, who also had been there. "Yes," he said thoughtfully, "it was amazing, wasn't it? But that's what compassion can do. It's the most healing of all human emotions. If we'd just let it, it could transform the world."

The truth is, this quality of compassion—and the word means "to suffer with"—*has* been transforming the world. And especially in the last century or two. It was the force that abolished slavery and put an end to child labor. It was the power that sent Florence Nightingale to Crimea and Albert Schweitzer to Africa. Mobilized in the March of Dimes, it helped to conquer polio. Without it there would be no Social Security, no Medicare, no SPCA, no Red Cross. But the most remarkable thing about it is what it can do to—and for—the person who feels it deeply.

Or even for the person who feels it suddenly and momentarily. Years ago, with two other college students, I was traveling one spring vacation in Spain. In Malaga we stayed in a *pensión* that was comfortable enough but strangely sombre. The owner, who spoke English, had little to say. His wife, a tall, tragic-looking woman, always wore black and never smiled. In the living room an enormous grand piano stood silent. The little Spanish maid told us that the Señora had been a concert pianist, but that two years ago her only child had died. She hadn't touched the piano since.

One afternoon we three American youngsters visited a *bodega,* a wine cellar where sherry was stored. The affable proprietor urged us to sample various vintages, which we were not at all reluctant to do, and we sang and danced all the way home. Back at the house, full of thoughtless gaiety, one of my friends sat down at the great piano, flung back the dusty keyboard cover, and began to play, very badly, while we supported him at the top of our lungs.

Suddenly the maid rushed into the room, looking appalled. Behind her came the owner, hands outstretched in a pleading gesture. "No, no," he cried. "You mustn't!" At the same instant another door opened, and there stood the Señora herself, dark, tragic eyes fixed on us. The music died. For an endless moment, all of us were frozen with dismay and embarrassment. Then suddenly this woman saw how miserable we were. She smiled, and great warmth and beauty came into her face. She walked forward, pushed my friend aside, sat down and began to play.

I remember how the maid hid her face in her hands, how the husband looked as if he wanted to burst into tears. The Señora kept playing, magnificent, soaring music that filled the whole house, driving the grief and the shadows away. And young though I was, I knew that she was free—free because she had felt pity for us, and the warmth of compassion had melted the ice around her heart.

Look around and you can see this healing force at work in all sorts of situations, large and small. One day last summer, hiking with two of the children through the hills of north Georgia, I came to a tiny cabin clinging to a rocky ledge. Behind a picket fence a white-haired mountain woman was working in her garden. When we stopped to admire her flowers, she told us that she lived there all alone. My city-bred youngsters regarded her with wonder. "How," asked one, "do you keep from being lonesome?" "Oh," she said, "if that feeling starts to come on in the summertime, I take a bunch of flowers to some shut-in. And if it's winter, I just go out and feed the birds!" An act of compassion—that was her instinctive antidote for loneliness. And it made her immune.

Where does it come from—this capacity to share another's grief or feel another's pain? I remember once asking a wise old minister about the most famous of all compassion stories: the Parable of The Good Samaritan. How did the Samaritan get that way, I wanted to know; what made him sensitive and responsive to the needs of the wounded man when the other travelers who saw that crumpled figure on the road to Jericho simply "passed by on the other side"?

"I think," the old clergyman replied, "there were three things that made him the way he was—qualities latent in all of us if only we'd work harder to develop and strengthen them. The first was *empathy*—the imaginative projection of one's own consciousness into another being. When the Samaritan saw the bandits' victim lying there, he didn't merely observe him, he identified with him, he became a part of him. This identification was so strong that you might almost say that when he went to help the man, he was helping the compassionate part of himself.

"The second thing he had was *courage,* and he needed it because it takes courage to care—and to translate caring into action. The ones who passed by on the other side were afraid, afraid of anything strange or challenging, afraid of getting involved, afraid the robbers might come back. The Samaritan had the courage to push those fears aside.

"The third thing I'm sure he had was the *habit of helping.* Going to the aid of the man on the Jericho road was no isolated incident in the Samaritan's life. He did what he did because he was the kind of man he was—and he didn't get that way overnight. Through the years he had trained himself to respond affirmatively to other people's needs. How? In the same way that any of us can do it, not so much by drastic self-discipline or heroic sacrifice as by the endless repetition of small effort. By going the extra mile —occasionally. By giving someone in trouble a hand—if you can. By taking a fair share of civic responsibilities —when you can manage it. These things may not seem to add up to much. But one day you may look around and discover that to an astonishing degree self has been pushed off its lonely and arrogant throne and—almost without knowing it—you have become a Samaritan yourself."

Empathy, courage, the habit of helping—perhaps the old minister was right. And perhaps there are still other qualities hidden in the deep tenderness that we call compassion. Whatever they are, we would do well to seek them in ourselves and encourage them in others—because without this quiet power there would be little hope for tomorrow.

Beautiful Dreamer

You know, when things are going pretty well at last, and the pressure is off, and you're not frightened anymore, sometimes you look back. You look back at all the misery and uncertainty, at the times when it was really rough, when you didn't think you could keep going for another day or even another hour. You expect to feel a great relief.

But you don't. You feel a kind of sadness—almost a sort of regret—a sense of loss rather than gain. Because you begin to realize that those times—grim though they were—had a vividness, a reality far more intense than the easier present. And it takes only a word, or a gesture, or a few notes from an old song to bring it all flooding back . . . .

We were broke that summer, good and broke. I had worked up enough courage to quit the magazine and try free-lancing, but I underestimated the length of time it takes to get started. Also, when you're scared you tighten up and write badly. We kept the show on the road by selling a few things—household things—at the outdoor auction on the edge of town. But that was all we did sell, and finally it got to the point where Pam decided to take the children to visit their grandmother for a while. We hadn't quarreled, or anything. It was just a question of debts, and of paying for the groceries.

She left early one morning, and I think that was the

longest day of my life. I tried to work, but it was no good; the house was too quiet and empty. I kept telling myself I didn't have to endure all this, that all I had to do was call the magazine and ask for my old job back. I was pretty sure I'd get it. In the end, it wasn't courage that kept me from making that call. It was lack of it. I didn't have the nerve to admit that I had failed.

The sun went down and the twilight was gray with loneliness. When it was fully dark, I decided to walk down to the auction and sell a suitcase I had. Pam had a birthday coming up and I wanted to buy her a present.

It wasn't much of a place, really, just a big shed full of junk, and a tent with folding chairs where people came to bid for things you'd have thought nobody could possibly want. Secondhand things, castoffs—even broken things.

The owner was a hard-bitten little gnome named Willie Madden who looked at the world suspiciously from under a green eyeshade and from behind a dead cigar. He and Pam had gotten pretty chummy over our previous transactions, but I didn't like him much.

I arranged to have the suitcase auctioned. Then, since there was an hour to kill, I prowled around looking at the old furniture and chipped china and musty books. And finally, near the back of the shed, I noticed a young couple standing close together and whispering about something.

They were not a very striking pair; neither of them was tall and the girl wasn't particularly pretty. But there was something nice and close about them. They were inspecting a secondhand baby carriage, and it was obvious that before long they were going to need one.

"Well, go and ask him," the girl said, loud enough for me to hear. "You can ask, can't you?"

The boy nodded and went away. While he was gone, the girl stood looking down at the carriage. In its prime it had been quite a fancy affair, and it was still in good condition. I saw her stroke the ivory handle gently, and once she bent and reexamined the price tag, as if she hoped somehow her first impression of what it read had been wrong.

Her husband came back presently with Willie Madden. Willie grunted at me from under his eyeshade, then went over and looked at the tag himself. "That's right," he said. "Twenty-five bucks. An absolute steal at that price, too. It's worth fifty."

The girl asked a question, her face wistful as she looked at the carriage.

"Well, bring it in, bring it in," Willie said impatiently. "Bring in anything you want to get rid of. But you better hurry. I got to be up on that platform in just forty-five minutes."

The youngsters hurried away, but in twenty minutes they were back. I watched them go up to Willie's cluttered desk and put down the things they were carrying: a fishing rod, a couple of dresses, an alarm clock, and a few other odds and ends including something that looked like a music box. It didn't look like twenty-five dollars' worth of auctionable stuff to me, and I knew it didn't to Willie. He poked at the music box with one skeptical finger. "This thing work?"

"It plays one tune," the girl said. "It's supposed to play three but it plays one."

Willie's cigar revolved slowly. "I paid twenty-two bucks for that carriage. Here it is, right in the book. If we can get that much for this stuff of yours, you can have it. But I tell you right now, I don't think you'll get that much. So don't say I didn't warn you. Go on, now; wait in the tent. I got things to do."

They went, and I followed them. I sat where I could watch their faces. They held hands and waited.

Somebody got a good buy on my suitcase; it went for

fourteen dollars, and was worth forty. The youngsters' things were at the end of the list; it was late when Willie got around to them. The fishing rod brought three dollars, the dresses two each, the alarm clock, fifty cents. It was hopeless, absolutely hopeless. I tried not to look at them.

Willie picked up the music box. "Now this here," he said, "is a genuine antique. What's more, it really plays. Listen."

He pressed the lever. The box gave a faint purring sound; then it played. The song was Stephen Foster's "Beautiful Dreamer." It came tinkling out, slow and sad, the most haunting of all American folk songs, maybe of folk songs anywhere:

> Beautiful dreamer, wake unto me,
> Starlight and dewdrop are waiting for thee.

The tent was very still. The music went on, thin and clear and sweet, and somehow everything was in it—all the loneliness and the heartache and the things all of us want to say and never find the words. I looked at the young couple, and something in their faces made my throat feel tight.

The music stopped. "Well," said Willie, "what am I bid? Ten dollars? Anyone bid ten dollars?"

Silence again. I thought of the fourteen dollars I would be getting for my suitcase. Less commission. I thought about Pam and her birthday, too.

"Anybody bid five?" Willie sounded impatient. "Anybody bid five dollars for this genuine antique?"

I took a deep breath, opened my mouth and then miserably closed it again.

"Five dollars!" said a voice behind me. I looked around. It was a thin, shabby man with a carefully waxed mustache. I had seen him at auctions before, but I had never heard him bid on anything.

Even Willie seemed rather surprised. "Fi-dollazime bid . . . who'll make it ten? Ten dollars? Who'll make it eight?"

"Eight!" It was a little birdlike woman on the far side of the tent.

Every eye in the place swung back to the shabby man. He did not even hesitate. "Ten dollars!"

"Twelve!" cried his rival. She looked as if she didn't have twelve cents.

"*Twelve* I'm bid," yelled Willie. "Do I hear fifteen?"

There was a hush that seemed to go on forever. Fifteen dollars would do it for them, plus the money from their other things. The girl was very pale; she was holding her husband's hand so tightly that I saw him wince.

The shabby man stood up slowly. "Fifteen dollars!" he said with grand finality.

That did it. The music box was going—it was gone—*sold* to the gentleman with the mustache. For a moment the grim thought occurred to me that the gentleman might not have fifteen dollars. But no, he produced the money, gave it to Willie's assistant, took the box.

When the tent was empty, I went back into the shed. The baby carriage, I was glad to note, was gone. I collected my suitcase money and decided to treat myself to a cup of coffee. The truth was I didn't want to go back to my empty house. I went into the diner across the street and stopped just inside the door. The little birdlike lady and her rival with the mustache were sitting there, side by side, on a couple of stools.

I understood the whole thing, then. I went up to them and said sharply, as if I had a right to know, "Where's the music box?"

The owner of the mustache looked faintly startled. "The box?" he said. "Why, Willie's got it."

I turned to his companion. "How much did Willie pay you to bid against each other?"

She dunked a doughnut daintily. "Why, nothing," she said. "We were glad to do it, weren't we, Henry?"

"I suppose," I said, "that it was Willie's money you used to pay for it, too."

"Sure," said Henry. "Where would I get fifteen bucks for a music box? Willie just hates for people to know what a softie he is, that's all."

I left them there and went back to the shed where Willie sat at his desk. I guess he wore that eyeshade to make himself look tough. "Where's the box?" I asked.

He stared me right in the eye. "What box?"

"Come on, Willie," I said. "I know what you did. Where is it?"

The eyeshade moved an inch to the left. "In the cupboard there. Why?"

"I want you to hold it for me. I'll give you twenty bucks for it when I have the money."

Willie leaned back in his chair. "Now just what," he said, "would you do with that box?"

"I'd give it to Pam for her birthday."

Willie shook his head. "Are you crazy? It's not worth five bucks, let alone twenty. It only plays one tune. It's supposed to play three."

"I like the tune it does play," I told him. "There's a lot of love in it."

"Love?" said Willie. He got up slowly and came around the desk. He looked at me balefully. "Why don't you get a job and do some work for a change? Why don't you quit this fool way of living?"

I just laughed out loud. I felt happy and warm and good inside. I knew that sooner or later everything would be all right.

Willie opened the cupboard. "Here." He held out the box. "Give it to Pam. On her birthday. From me."

I hesitated for a second; then I took it. There are times when it is selfish to refuse a gift. "Thanks."

"Well, go on home," said Willie. "I can't stand around here all night talking."

So I went home. The house was still dark and empty, but I put the box on the table by our bed. I put it there, and I let it play, and I wasn't lonely any more.

Watch Out for Charm

In the past century or two, down here in the Deep South, we've managed to get rid of a respectable number of nuisances. Yellow fever and carpetbaggers are no more. Mosquitoes have mellowed; so have rural sheriffs. But one velvet trap still awaits the unwary visitor: the subtle, insidious, silken snare of charm.

As you may have noticed with some dismay, most Southerners would rather be charming than rich. They believe that you can devote your energies to making money or to being delightful, but you can't really do both. When faced with the choice, they don't even hesitate, because some ancient ancestral instinct whispers that charm will get a charmer all sorts of things that money can't begin to buy.

I had forgotten how pervasive and powerful this life-style is until I moved back to my hometown—Savannah—after several uneasy years in the North. In this languorous old seaport, the output of charm per capita is unbelievable. Visitors are often struck by such a deluge of it that they go bobbing around, dazed and helpless, like bewildered cherries in a sea of whipped cream. When there *are* no visitors, Savannahians keep in practice by charming one another.

At first, exposure to such expert charmers can be delightful. You feel flattered, uplifted, bemused, and enchanted. You never dreamed that you were so good-looking, so witty, so irresistible. It takes a while for the dark realization to creep in that, as a matter of fact, you're not.

I discovered—or rather, rediscovered—this within forty-eight hours of my return. It was a golden Sunday morning. On the church steps I met a friend of my mother's, a tall lady in a flowered hat who took my hand and held it tenderly. "My dear," she said (a warning bell should have clanged, because I wasn't even remotely "her dear"), "my dear, I've never seen you looking so young. Or so handsome. You certainly do brighten the day!"

I went into church feeling quite exhilarated. A moment later, I came out looking for one of our children who was late. As I did, my eye fell upon an acquaintance I'd seen the night before whooping it up at a memorable party. He was tottering up the steps, bright red eyes in a pale green face. "My dear," my mother's friend was saying to him, "how marvelous you look! So smart! So debonair!" A howling hypocrite? Not at all. She was just being what she had been conditioned to be since the age of three. *Charmante.* No matter what.

I have a sharp-edged and cynical friend named Danforth (his mother was from Vermont) who takes a very dim view of charmers. A real charmer, my friend Danforth says, is an accomplished actor—that's all—with a trained actor's constant awareness of audience reaction. The main purpose of the act, he maintains, is not to make other people feel good; it's to draw favorable attention to the charmer. "God help anyone who marries one," he growls. "If a person goes around all day being charming, you can bet that when he comes home he'll snarl at his wife, cuff the kids, and kick the cat right through the ceiling."

There may be some truth in this. I once knew an elderly Savannahian who specialized in being charming to everyone. One day her pet abomination, the pastor of a rival church, came to call. She couldn't stand the man, but she smiled benignly, offered him tea, praised his sermons, lauded his piety, and admired his theology. When he left, she lay down on the sofa and had a fatal stroke. She was one of those women who have to be charming if it kills them, and by george, this time it did.

My friend Danforth says that Southerners are always confusing eccentricity with charm. He may be right about that, too. Consider, for example, my Great-Aunt Lavinia who was brought up around the turn of the century by three elderly members of our clan, all rather odd. Cousin Wayne, a bachelor who passionately admired the Wright brothers, spent most of his time experimenting with unsuccessful gliders. Maud and Muriel, his two maiden sisters, kept house for their brother and the orphaned Lavinia.

Every afternoon these formidable spinsters retired to their room in shuttered gloom and took a nap. Nothing under any circumstances was allowed to interfere with this solemn ritual. Silence had to reign. Poor Lavinia had to creep around the house like a wistful ghost.

One sultry afternoon in 1901 things began to come unglued. First a hitherto circumspect cat decided to have kittens in an antique Chinese bowl on the sideboard. This blessed event already had Lavinia somewhat unstrung when an irascible major who lived next door appeared, red-faced and furious, to report that Cousin Wayne, taking off from some undetermined pinnacle in his latest glider, had landed head down in his well. Somebody, the major said angrily, ought to get him out before he ruined the well. Frantic and trembling, Lavinia hurried outside to see if the report was true (it was). As she did, a wild-eyed newsboy cycling past flung an extra edition of the local paper at her feet. When she saw the headlines, something in Lavinia snapped. She rushed up to the sacred siesta room and flung open the door. "Wake up, wake up!" she screamed. "The cat's in the well, Cousin Wayne's having kittens, McKinley's been shot, and I can't stand everything!"

An impartial observer might have maintained that Great-Aunt Lavinia never really recovered. But it was widely held in the family that while she might not be over-burdened with brains, Lavinia was loaded with charm, a state of affairs that everyone agreed was much better.

About the highest compliment you can pay a Southerner is to say that he or she "could charm a bird out of a tree." (My friend Danforth says sourly that the tree is where the bird belongs, not in the clutches of the charmer.) But when you try to pin down the key ingredient, it's a little like trying to catch moonbeams in your hat.

The charming thing about charm is that it varies so as-tonishingly from individual to individual. What is rep-rehensible in one person can be beguiling in another.

Take my Aunt Jessamine, for example, who lived up in Charleston (South Carolina, of course). Nobody was more charming, but the awful truth is that much of her charm was based on the fact that whenever Aunt Jessamine wanted something she didn't beg or wheedle or cajole. She simply told dreadful lies.

I remember once being in an airport with Aunt Jes-samine when our flight to Charleston was canceled because of some trouble with the aircraft. All other carriers were booked solid. When I reported this to Aunt Jessamine, she went up to the ticket counter, clutched her throat, gave a sepulchral cough, and asked in fainting accents to see the manager. She was strong as a mule, and twice as healthy, but the next thing I knew we were flying to Charleston as emergency-illness cases. My conscience gnawed me all the way, but Aunt Jessamine felt just fine.

Then there was Aunt Harriet, whose charm lay in her infinite capacity for sharing gloom. People came from miles around to tell their troubles to Aunt Harriet. "Oh," she would say, shaking her head in commiseration and disbelief, "ain't it *awful?*" (She was capable of better grammar, but she liked the alliteration.) Aunt Harriet never tried to *solve* anyone's problems; that would have ruined everything. She just agonized over them—and people went away feeling much better.

Finally, of course, there was my Aunt Daisy, now revered by millions as Juliette Low, the founder of girl scouting in this country. Daisy's charm lay not so much in her eccentricities (of which she had plenty) as in the *reasons* she gave for doing or not doing something. My father once told me of the time in London, back in approximately the days of Sherlock Holmes, when he and Daisy were caught in a torrential rainstorm. Daisy stood in a doorway while her younger brother ran through the downpour looking for a hansom cab. When, half-drowned, he finally found one, Daisy refused to get into it because, she said, the horse had a scornful mouth.

"Did it really?" I asked, fascinated.

"Well, yes," my father said thoughtfully. "But I'm sure it wasn't being scornful of *us.*"

Daisy, who spent as much time in England as in America, always seemed to drive on the wrong side of the street no matter which country she was in. One day, taking violent evasive action as usual in her old Franklin, she collided with a house and came to rest in the dining room. Without a word to the flabbergasted family, she leaped from the car, sped to the corner drugstore, and called her brother Bill, who was a lawyer. "What did you say to those people?" cried Bill, fearing some ultra-incriminating admission. "Why, nothing," replied Daisy indignantly. "I didn't think it would be polite to interrupt them at lunch."

My wife, who has been reading some of this over my shoulder (one of her more char—I mean, friendly traits), points out that I have gotten completely off the track. "You started out to say why charm is so insidious," she says, "and here you are going on and on about your nutty old aunts."

Well, Southerners do have a tendency to go on and on. But if you want my final word, it's this: My friend Danforth is wrong. Charm isn't all playacting or self-centeredness. Charm is also a reaching out. It's a small voice saying, "Look, I'm aware of you. I know you're there. I want you to like me, sure—but I also want you to feel easier about yourself."

Call it charm, call it caring—it's something we need badly in this mechanized, fragmented, dehumanized world. Something to fall back on when we can't stand everything. So you-all come on down and *get* charmed. Won't hurt a bit. Might be good for everybody!

How Wonderful You Are!

Down in Georgia, some years ago, my mother moved out of the old house where our family had lived for almost a century and a half. It's astounding how much stuff can accumulate in the course of five or six generations. The cellar and attic were crammed with boxes and trunks full of an incredible assortment of odds and ends. And since she was moving to a much smaller place, my mother asked my sisters and me to look it over and get rid of most of it.

I began, I must confess, with visions of rare and valuable Confederate stamps dancing in my head, or possibly an autograph of Button Gwinnett, the shy delegate from Georgia who signed his name to the Declaration of Independence but hardly anywhere else—with the result that his signature is worth thousands of dollars today. It soon became evident, though, that all we had, really, was a mighty collection of antiquated junk. But I found something of value, all the same.

I found it in the letters, a whole trunkful of them. Most of them were written in faded ink and grimy with the dust of decades. We'd stand there in the shuttered gloom, ankle-deep in mismated spurs and andirons, in tarnished epaulets, and scraps of torn lace or faded brocade, and read a paragraph or two. And it was like listening to voices, faint and far away, echoing down the corridor of time.

The letters were never about great historical events. They weren't passionate love letters either. They simply chronicled the lives of ordinary people: parties and picnics, business successes or failures, pets, children, the weather. They might almost have been written by my sisters to me, or vice versa, except for one thing. The emotional restraints that have become part of our daily lives were largely lacking.

The people in those generations cared about one another, enormously and intimately. And they said so, with an emphasis that was perhaps naïve but was also deeply impressive. In a hundred different ways, they spoke of their love and admiration for one another, and you could feel their sincerity warm on the brittle paper:

> You don't know how much your visit meant to each of us! When you left, I felt as if the sun had stopped shining.

> The courage with which you are facing your difficulties is an inspiration to all of us. We haven't the slightest doubt that in the end you will triumph over all of them.

> Have I told you lately what a wonderful person you are? Never forget how much your friends and family love and admire you.

How wonderful you are! That was the steady refrain, and it made me stop and think. In each of these people, no doubt, there had been much that could have been criticized. But when you remembered the times they had lived through —the war that ended for them in poverty and bitterness and defeat, the terrifying epidemics of yellow fever—it was impossible to escape the conclusion that the writers of these letters were stronger than we are—that they faced greater tests with greater fortitude. And where did they get that strength? The answer lay in my dusty hands. They got it from one another.

Never forget how much you are loved and admired.

There it was: the faith, the encouragement, these strands of reassurance woven into a powerful network of mutual support. Nobody had to face anything without allies whose loyalty was beyond question. Nobody was ever alone.

Such loyalty and affection were implicit in my own family relationships, I knew, but they were seldom expressed, and certainly not in such a forthright way. Somewhere along the line, my generation had put a checkrein on the release of such emotions. To give utterance to them had become corny, somehow faintly foolish. It was out of fashion; it just wasn't done. I don't pretend to know what brought this change about, but I do know this: It seriously interferes with one of the deepest of all human needs—the desire for acceptance and approval by other people.

Knowing that he is loved, the individual does not have to worry about acceptance or approval—he's got them. Knowing that he is admired, his self-confidence remains high.

If other people believe that he can cope with his difficulties, then the fear of failure (the most paralyzing of all fears) recedes and diminishes. The converse is also true. It has been said that you tend to become what you think you are. But what you think you are is colored, inevitably, by what you conceive other people's opinion of you to be. If you think they are critical (or even indifferent), your self-esteem shrinks, and with it your capacity for living.

Some criticism, no doubt, is constructive, but too much is a subtle poison. A friend of mine told me of a club he belonged to in his undergraduate days at the University of Wisconsin. The members were a group of brilliant boys, some with real literary talent. At each meeting one of them would read a story or essay he had written and submit it to the criticism of the others. No punches were pulled; each manuscript was mercilessly dissected. The sessions were so brutal that the club members dubbed themselves *The Stranglers.* This club was strictly a masculine affair, so naturally the coeds formed a comparable group of their own known as *The Wranglers.* They, too, read their manuscripts aloud. But the criticism was much gentler. In fact, there was almost none at all. The Wranglers hunted for kind things to say. All efforts, however feeble, were encouraged.

The payoff came about twenty years later, when some alumnus made an analysis of his classmates' careers. Of all the bright young talent in The Stranglers, not one had made a literary reputation of any kind. Out of The Wranglers had come half a dozen successful writers, some of national prominence, led by Marjorie Kinnan Rawlings, who wrote *The Yearling.* Coincidence? Hardly. The amount of basic talent in the two groups was much the same. But The Wranglers gave one another a lift. The Stranglers promoted self-criticism, self-disparagement, self-doubt. In choosing a name for themselves, they had been wiser than they knew.

Awareness of the power of affection to unlock human capabilities is at least two thousand years old ("A new commandment I give unto you, That ye love one another . . ."). But affection is not much good unless it is expressed. What's more, I have a notion that unexpressed feelings have a tendency to shrink, wither, and ultimately die. Putting an emotion into words gives it a life and a reality that otherwise it doesn't have.

Reading those old letters left me with the uncomfortable feeling that in this department of living we are far less wise than our ancestors. I would say that, on the whole, modern men are worse offenders than modern women. They have arrived, somehow, at the conviction that it is unmanly to show emotion. Most wives, I'm sure, complain at some time or another about the lack of endearments, of the small romantic gestures that were so common in the courtship period. To which the husband is likely to reply:

"You know perfectly well I love you. Why do I have to keep proving it all the time?"

Being more intuitive than her life-companion, the wife knows that affection is not a static thing, that it either increases or decreases, and that stating it now and then gives it a chance to grow and expand.

Similarly, expressing confidence in a person's ability to accomplish something actually strengthens that ability. Once, visiting a college classmate who has made an outstanding mark in life, I happened to open a book in his library. It was a birthday gift from his mother, and it was inscribed: WITH LOVE AND PRIDE FOR MY SON, WHO HAS DONE GREAT THINGS AND WILL DO GREATER YET. I was reminded of this the other day when Charles Dumas became the first athlete to high-jump seven feet. His mother, apparently, was not surprised. "I just told him" she said later, "to go out there and jump seven feet!" Whereupon he rose, you might say, to the occasion.

Emerson, that incredible old nutshell-putter, has said, "Our chief want in life is, somebody who shall make us do what we can." He might have added that the best method for this somebody to use would be simply to expect us to achieve and then let us know about it. The human animal is a strange creature: It will often make more of an effort to please someone else than it will to please itself.

The expression of affection does a lot, I think, for the person who expresses it; people who give admiration and affection get them back—if what they give is spontaneous and sincere. People are irresistibly drawn to "warm" people. And what is a warm person, except one who instinctively takes the checkrein off his emotions and enthusiasms when dealing with people he cares about? Such warmth is contagious. If even one member of an indifferent family can recapture it, it will spread imperceptibly to the others, until the decline of intimacy is halted.

So, while I found no valuable stamps or rare autographs in those dusty trunks in the attic, I took away a legacy in the form of a question to ask myself from time to time. To be manifestly loved, to be openly admired are human needs as basic as breathing. Why, then, wanting them so much ourselves, do we deny them so often to others?

Why, indeed?

2

The Gift of Shared Wisdom

It was my lot in life to have more schooling than most. Four years at a great American university, two more at a famous British one. I'm not at all sure that I took proper advantage of my opportunities. I resolutely chose courses I liked and avoided those I didn't, especially any that smelled of mathematics. I studied enough to get by, but I also spent a tremendous amount of time (it seems to me now) playing bridge, going to the movies, working at odd jobs (I had to earn most of my expenses), and rowing around various bodies of water in eight-oared shells.

I suppose during those six years of higher education *some* knowledge seeped in. But not much wisdom. Not much that really changed my outlook or my values or my goals in life. Those basic things were affected more by certain chance encounters I had than by anything I read in books.

In those rare encounters a spark would jump from another person to me. Usually the other person was older, wiser, more experienced, and willing to share certain insights or attitudes. The setting was never academic although, as you'll see, one of these persons was a teacher. Actually, I don't think the setting made any difference. The spark jumped, or it didn't.

When it did, it left me changed.

Here are some of those encounters, as I remember them.

The Stranger Who Taught Magic

That July morning, I remember, was like any other, calm and opalescent before the heat of the fierce Georgia sun. I was 13, sunburned, shaggy-haired, a little aloof, and solitary. In winter I had to put on shoes and go to school like everyone else. But summers I lived by the sea, and my mind was empty and wild and free.

On this particular morning, I had tied my rowboat to the pilings of an old dock upriver from our village. There, sometimes, the striped sheepshead lurked in the still, green water. I was crouched, motionless as a stone, when a voice spoke suddenly above my head: "Canst thou draw out leviathan with a hook? or his tongue with a cord which thou lettest down?"

I looked up, startled, into a lean pale face and a pair of the most remarkable eyes I had ever seen. It wasn't a question of color; I'm not sure, now, what color they were. It was a combination of things: warmth, humor, interest, alertness. *Intensity*—that's the word, I guess—and, underlying it all, a curious kind of mocking sadness. I believe I thought him old.

He saw how taken aback I was. "Sorry," he said. "It's a bit early in the morning for the Book of Job, isn't it?" He nodded at the two or three fish in the boat. "Think you could teach me how to catch those?"

Ordinarily, I was wary of strangers, but anyone interested in fishing was hardly a stranger. I nodded, and he climbed down into the boat. "Perhaps we should introduce ourselves," he said. "But then again, perhaps not. You're a boy willing to teach, I'm a teacher willing to learn. That's introduction enough. I'll call you *Boy,* and you call me *Sir.*"

Such talk sounded strange in my world of sun and salt water. But there was something so magnetic about the man, and so disarming about his smile, that I didn't care.

I gave him a hand line and showed him how to bait his hooks with fiddler crabs. He kept losing baits, because he could not recognize a sheepshead's stealthy tug, but he seemed content not to catch anything. He told me he had rented one of the weathered bungalows behind the dock. "I needed to hide for a while," he said. "Not from the police, or anything like that. Just from friends and relatives. So don't tell anyone you've found me, will you?"

I was tempted to ask where he was from; there was a crispness in the way he spoke that was very different from the soft accents I was accustomed to. But I didn't. He had said he was a teacher, though, and so I asked what he taught.

"In the school catalog they call it English," he said. "But I like to think of it as a course in magic—in the mystery and magic of words. Are you fond of words?"

I said that I had never thought much about them. I also pointed out that the tide was ebbing, that the current was too strong for more fishing, and that in any case it was time for breakfast.

"Of course," he said, pulling in his line. "I'm a little forgetful about such things these days." He eased himself back onto the dock with a little grimace, as if the effort cost him something. "Will you be back on the river later?"

I said that I would probably go casting for shrimp at low tide.

"Stop by," he said. "We'll talk about words for a while,

and then perhaps you can show me how to catch shrimp."

So began a most unlikely friendship, because I did go back. To this day, I'm not sure why. Perhaps it was because, for the first time, I had met an adult on terms that were in balance. In the realm of words and ideas, he might be the teacher. But in my own small universe of winds and tides and sea creatures, the wisdom belonged to me.

Almost every day after that, we'd go wherever the sea gods or my whim decreed. Sometimes up the silver creeks, where the terrapin skittered down the banks and the great blue herons stood like statues. Sometimes along the ocean dunes, fringed with graceful sea oats, where by night the great sea turtles crawled and by day the wild goats browsed. I showed him where the mullet swirled and where the flounder lay in cunning camouflage. I learned that he was incapable of much exertion; even pulling up the anchor seemed to exhaust him. But he never complained. And, all the time, talk flowed from him like a river.

Much of it I have forgotten now, but some comes back as clear and distinct as if it all happened yesterday, not decades ago. We might be sitting in a hollow of the dunes, watching the sun go down in a smear of crimson. "Words," he'd say. "Just little black marks on paper. Just sounds in the empty air. But think of the power they have! They can make you laugh or cry, love or hate, fight or run away. They can heal or hurt. They even come to look and sound like what they mean. Angry looks angry on the page. Ugly sounds ugly when you say it. Here!" He would hand me a piece of shell. "Write a word that looks or sounds like what it means."

I would stare helplessly at the sand.

"Oh," he'd cry, "you're being dense. There are so many! Like *whisper* . . . *leaden* . . . *twilight* . . . *chime*. Tell you what: When you go to bed tonight, think of five words that look like what they mean and five that sound like what they mean. Don't go to sleep until you do!"

And I would try—but always fall asleep.

Or we might be anchored just offshore, casting into the surf for sea bass, our little bateau nosing over the rollers like a restless hound. "Rhythm," he would say. "Life is full of it; words should have it, too. But you have to train your ear. Listen to the waves on a quiet night; you'll pick up the cadence. Look at the patterns the wind makes in dry sand and you'll see how syllables in a sentence should fall. Do you know what I mean?"

My conscious self didn't know; but perhaps something deep inside me did. In any case, I listened.

I listened, too, when he read from the books he sometimes brought: Kipling, Conan Doyle, Tennyson's *Idylls of the King*. Often he would stop and repeat a phrase or a line that pleased him. One day, in Malory's *Le Morte d'Arthur,* he found one: "And the great horse grimly neighed." "Close your eyes," he said to me, "and say that slowly, out loud." I did. "How did it make you feel?" "It gives me the shivers," I said truthfully. He was delighted.

But the magic that he taught was not confined to words; he had a way of generating in me an excitement about things I had always taken for granted. He might point to a bank of clouds. "What do you see there? Colors? That's not enough. Look for towers and drawbridges. Look for dragons and griffins and strange and wonderful beasts."

Or he might pick up an angry claw-brandishing blue crab, holding it cautiously by the back flippers as I had taught him. "Pretend you're this crab," he'd say. "What do you see through those stalklike eyes? What do you feel with those complicated legs? What goes on in your tiny brain? Try it for just five seconds. Stop being a boy. Be a crab!"

And I would stare in amazement at the furious creature, feeling my comfortable identity lurch and sway under the impact of the idea. So the days went by. Our excursions became less frequent, because he tired so easily. He brought two chairs down to the dock and some books, but he didn't read much. He seemed content to watch me as I fished, or the circling gulls, or the slow river coiling past.

A sudden shadow fell across my life when my parents told me I was going to camp for two weeks. On the dock that afternoon I asked my friend if he would be there when I got back. "I hope so," he said gently.

But he wasn't. I remember standing on the sun-warmed planking of the old dock, staring at the shuttered bungalow and feeling a hollow sense of finality and loss. I ran to Jackson's grocery store—where everyone knew everything—and asked where the schoolteacher had gone.

"He was sick, real sick," Mrs. Jackson replied. "Doc phoned his relatives up north to come get him. He left something for you—he figured you'd be asking for him."

She handed me a book. It was a slender volume of verse, *Flame and Shadow,* by someone I had never heard of: Sara Teasdale. The corner of one page was turned down, and there was a penciled star by one of the poems. I still have the book, with the poem "On the Dunes."

> If there is any life when death is over,
> These tawny beaches will know much of me,
> I shall come back, as constant and as changeful
> As the unchanging, many-colored sea.
> If life was small, if it has made me scornful,
> Forgive me; I shall straighten like a flame
> In the great calm of death, and if you want me
> Stand on the sea-ward dunes and call my name.

Well, I have never stood on the dunes and called his name. For one thing, I never knew it; for another, I'd be too self-conscious. And there are long stretches when I forget all about him. But sometimes—when the music or the magic in a phrase makes my skin tingle, or when I pick up an angry blue crab, or when I see a dragon in the flaming sky—sometimes I remember.

Interview With an Immortal

The month was June, the English weather was blue and gold. The world was young, and so was I. But, driving down from Oxford in the old Sunbeam I had borrowed for the occasion, I felt my assurance deserting me.

The great man was almost a recluse now, and it was said that he did not care for Americans. Through a mutual friend I had managed to secure permission to visit him. Now as I neared the little village of Burwash, where he lived, I began to experience something like stage fright. And when I found the sombre seventeenth-century house and saw my host walking down to the gate to meet me, I grew so flustered that I hardly knew whether to shake hands or turn and run.

He was so small! The crown of the floppy hat he wore was not much higher than my shoulder, and I doubt if he weighed 120 pounds. His skin was dark for an Englishman's; his mustache was almost white. His eyebrows were as thick and tangled as marsh grass, but behind the gold-rimmed glasses his eyes were as bright as a terrier's. He was sixty-nine years old.

He saw instantly how ill at ease I was. "Come in, come in," he said companionably, opening the gate. "I was just going to inspect my navy." A Scottie came bounding down the path and stopped short when he saw me. "Now, this," his master said, "is Malachi. He's really quite friendly. But of course, being a Scot, he hates to show it."

He led me, still speechless, to a pond at the end of the garden, and there was the so-called navy: a six-foot skiff with hand-cranked paddle wheels. "You can be the engine room," he said. "I'll be the passenger list."

I was so agitated that I cranked too hard. The paddle wheel broke and there I was, marooned in the middle of a fishpond with Rudyard Kipling. He began to laugh, and so did I, and the ice was broken.

A gardener finally rescued us with a long rake. By then my host had me talking. There was something about him that drove the shyness out of you, a kind of understanding that went deeper than words and set up an instantaneous closeness. It was odd; we couldn't have been more different. He was British; I was American. He was near the end of an illustrious road; I was at the beginning of an obscure one. He had had years of ill health and pain; I was untouched by either. He knew nothing about me—there was nothing to know. I knew all about him, and so to me he was not just a fragile little man in a toy boat. He was Kim and Fuzzy-Wuzzy and Gunga Din. He was Danny Deever and the Elephant's Child. He was the dawn coming up like thunder on the road to Mandalay; he was the rough laughter of the barrack room, the chatter of the bazaar and the great organ tones of "Recessional." To me he was, quite simply, a miracle, and no doubt this showed in my dazzled eyes, and he felt it and was warmed by it.

I had had an ulterior motive in coming, of course. I wanted to meet him for himself, but I was also a puzzled and unsure young man. I had in my pocket a letter offering me a job as instructor in an American university. I didn't really want to be a teacher; I knew I didn't have the selflessness or the patience. What I wanted to be, ultimately, was a writer. But the teaching job was the only offer I had. I had no other prospects, no money at all. At home, the dead hand of the

Great Depression still lay heavy on the land. Should I play it safe, and say yes to the offer?

What I wanted desperately was for someone of great wisdom and experience in the field of letters to tell me what to do. But I knew this was a preposterous responsibility to thrust upon a stranger. And so I waited, hoping that somehow the heavens would open and the miracle of certainty would descend upon me.

While I waited, he talked. And, as he talked, I began to forget about my problems. He tossed words into the air, and they flashed like swords. He spoke of his friendship with Cecil Rhodes, through whose generosity I had gone to Oxford. "They say we were both imperialists," said Kipling a little grimly. "Well, maybe we were. The word is out of fashion now, and some Englishmen are weak enough to be ashamed of it. I'm not." He questioned me almost sharply about some poets of prominence: Eliot, Stein, Cummings. I said I thought they were good.

"Do you?" he asked guilelessly. "Quote me a few lines."

I sat there, helpless, and he laughed. "You see," he said, "that's the trouble with verse that doesn't rhyme. But let's not be too harsh where poets are concerned. They have to live in no-man's-land, halfway between dreams and reality."

"Like Mowgli," I said impulsively, thinking of the brown-skinned boy torn between village and jungle.

He gave me a look with his blue eyes. "Like most of us," he said.

He talked of ambition, of how long it took fully to master any art or craft. And of secondary ambitions: the more you had, he said, the more fully you lived. "I always wanted to build or buy a 400-ton brig," he said reflectively, "and sail her round the world. Never did. Now, I suppose, it's too late." He lit a cigarette and looked at me through the smoke. "Do the things you really want to do if you possibly can.

Don't wait for circumstances to be exactly right. You'll find that they never are.

"My other unrealized ambition," he went on, "was to be an archaeologist. For sheer, gem-studded romance, no other job can touch it. Why, right under our feet here in Sussex . . . ."

He described how he had decided to sink a well. A few feet down, they found a Jacobean tobacco pipe. Below that, a Cromwellian latten spoon. Still farther down, a Roman horse bit. And, finally, water.

We went back to his study, a large square room lined with bookcases on two sides. There were his desk, his chair, an enormous wastebasket and his pens—the kind you dip in ink. At right angles to the fireplace was a small sofa. "I lie there," he said with a smile, "and wait for my daemon to tell me what to do."

"Daemon?"

He shrugged. "Intuition. Subconscious. Whatever you want to call it."

"Can you always hear him?"

"No," he said slowly. "Not always. But I learned long ago that it's best to wait until you do. When your daemon says nothing, he usually means no."

Mrs. Kipling called us to lunch, and afterward I felt I should take my leave. But Kipling would not hear of it. "I'm still full of talk," he said. "You've eaten my salt, so now you must be my audience."

So we talked. Or rather, he talked while I made superhuman efforts to remember everything. He had a way of thrusting a harsh truth at you and then, in the next breath, beguiling you into a wry acceptance of it. "If you're endowed," he said at one point, "with any significant energies or talent, you may as well resign yourself to the fact that throughout your life you will be carrying coattail riders who will try to exploit you. But instead of fuming and fretting about this you'd better thank God for the qualities that attract the parasites, and not waste time trying to shake them off."

We talked of friendship; he thought young ones were best and lasted longest. "When you're young," he said, "you're not afraid to give yourself away. You offer warmth and vitality and sympathy without thinking. Later on, you begin to weigh what you give."

I said, somewhat diffidently, that he was giving me a lot, and his eyes twinkled. "A fair exchange. You're giving me attention. That's a form of affection, you know."

Looking back, I think he knew that in my innocence I was eager to love everything and please everybody, and he was trying to warn me not to lose my own identity in the process. Time after time he came back to this theme. "The individual has always had to struggle to keep from being overwhelmed by the tribe. To be your own man is a hard business. If you try it, you'll be lonely often, and sometimes frightened. But no price is too high to pay for the privilege of owning yourself."

Suddenly the shadows were long on the grass. When I stood up to go, I remembered the letter in my pocket and the advice I had thought I wanted. But now there was nothing to ask. *Do the things you really want to do . . . . Don't wait for circumstances to be exactly right . . . . When your daemon says nothing, he usually means no . . . . No price is too high to pay for the privilege of owning yourself.*

I knew, now, that I would refuse the teaching job and wait for my daemon to speak clearly to me.

We walked to the gate, Malachi scampering ahead of us. My host held out his hand. "Thank you," he said. "You've done me good."

The thought that I could have done anything for him was beyond my grasp. I thanked him and climbed into the old Sunbeam. I looked back once. He was still standing there in his floppy hat, a great little man who forgot his own illness and his own problems and spent a whole day trying to help a troubled and self-conscious boy from across the sea.

He had a gift for young friendships, all right. He gave me much more than advice. He gave me a little bit of himself to carry away. After all these years, I feel the warmth of it still.

On the Far Side of Failure

At the age when you're convinced you can twist the world into a pretzel, I left my native Georgia and got a job, a very small job, on a New York magazine. I intended to be a writer. I figured that I would learn exactly what sort of writing was in demand; then I would quit my job, start producing reams of this precious commodity, and shortly retire to the Riviera to hobnob with Noel Coward and Somerset Maugham.

It didn't quite work out this way. The things I wrote at night or on weekends came bouncing back with dismal regularity. At the end of a year the record showed nothing but consistent failure.

Well, if I wasn't cut out to be a writer, I told myself, I could at least take over the magazine business. To hasten this process, every noon I would go to the Automat, buy a bun, take it out to a bench in Central Park, and dream great dreams.

One day, munching on my bun, I began to wonder why my employer, who owned a whole flock of magazines, didn't translate some of his better magazine articles into Spanish, combine them into a single top-quality magazine, and assign a star salesman—me—to sell it all over Latin America. It was such a splendid vision that I arose with a shout, scattered my bun crumbs to the startled pigeons, and hurried back to my cubbyhole at the office.

Of course, there might be problems in the form of tariffs,

currency regulations, and so on. Before approaching the boss with my brilliant idea, I decided to find out about these details. I asked my cell mate at the office if he knew of an authority on Latin America.

"Latin America?" he said. "I guess T. J. Watson over at IBM knows as much about Latin America as anyone. They do tremendous business down there."

"IBM?" I echoed. "What's that?" I thought it might be a federal agency like the WPA, which was flourishing at the time.

He gave me a look of weary scorn. "International Business Machines. Why don't you go back to Georgia?"

Well, I had never heard of International Business Machines, or this T. J. Watson either. But certainly he had to eat, and if I was careful, I figured, I could afford two buns in the park—or maybe even the cafeteria at the zoo.

So I called up IBM and asked for Mr. Watson. When a secretarial voice answered, I announced cheerily that I would like to buy Mr. Watson a lunch and pick his brains about Latin America. I'd been told he was an authority, I explained. Friday would suit me best. (It was payday.) We would eat in the park, I said, not specifying the menu. I could pick Mr. Watson up at his office, or we could meet at the zoo.

"The zoo?" echoed the voice, with rising inflection.

"The cafeteria at the Central Park Zoo," I said a bit impatiently. "Will you go and ask him, please?"

The voice went away, but soon came back. Mr. Watson would be glad to see me, it said. But he had suggested that I come and have lunch with him. In the light of my finances, this struck me as a first-rate suggestion.

When I walked into the IBM skyscraper on Fifty-seventh Street and asked the elevator starter if he happened to know on which floor someone named T. J. Watson worked, he gave me a queer look and a number. On the designated floor, the receptionist summoned a secretary who took me to a waiting room. There another secretary came and escorted me to another waiting room. Each time the paneling grew darker and richer, the pile of the carpet deeper, and the reverential silence more profound. So did my conviction that somebody was making a terrible mistake —probably me.

The final secretary was a man. "The president will see you now," he said pleasantly.

"President?" I said hoarsely. But already a massive door had swung open, revealing an office roughly the size of Grand Central Station. At the far end, behind an enormous, polished desk, was a tall, silver-haired gentleman: Thomas J. Watson, Senior, one of the mightiest tycoons in America. On his desk was a small, neatly lettered sign. THINK, it said. I *was* thinking—thinking I should have stayed in Georgia.

He rose with as much courtesy as if I had been a visiting ambassador. "Well, young man," he said, "it's nice of you to drop in. Sit down and tell me what I can do for you."

I moved forward like a man in a trance and sat down. But I was speechless.

He waved his hand. "Don't let these surroundings bother you. When I was about your age, I was working in a store in an upstate town named Painted Post, trying to sell pianos and organs. Backgrounds change, but people don't—much. Now tell me: What's all this about Latin America?"

My voice came back from wherever it had gone, and I told him about my plan. He listened attentively. I said that I wanted to know what difficulties to expect.

He nodded. "It's not a bad idea at all. I'll arrange for you to see the right people after lunch." He touched a button, and a little man appeared with a notebook. On the notebook cover, I noticed, was a word stamped in gold: THINK.

Mr. Watson named the people I was to see. "And while you're at it," he added casually, "see that this young man gets a copy of every magazine published in Latin America." (They came, too. In droves.)

"Now," said Mr. Watson, "how about some lunch? I really was tempted to meet you at the zoo. Nobody ever asked me to the zoo for lunch before. But we have our own dining rooms here, and the habit of time-saving is hard to break."

Mr. Watson and I had a fine lunch. He told me about IBM, its vast worldwide organization, the benefits for employes, the little copybook maxims that he liked to hang on office and factory walls. People didn't notice them consciously after a while, he admitted, but unconsciously they were affected by them. THINK was one of his favorites. AIM HIGH was another. "You were aiming pretty high," he said quizzically, "when you said you wanted to pick my brains. But I like that. That's why I said yes."

I admitted, with a gulp, that when I walked into the building I hadn't the faintest idea who he was. He laughed. "It's a blow to my ego, but probably a healthy one." He looked at me speculatively. "How much salary are you making now?"

I told him. It didn't take long.

He smiled. "If you'd like to join our IBM family, I think we could do a little better for you than that."

"Thank you, sir," I said, "but machines don't like me. What I want to be eventually is . . ." I stopped. I had about decided that I would never be a writer. But I had a feeling that this man could see right through me anyway, so I told him about the year of writing failures, the endless rejection slips.

He leaned back in his chair. "It's not exactly my line," he said, "but would you like me to give you a formula for writing success?" He hesitated. "It's quite simple, really. Double your rate of failure."

I stared at him. This was no copybook maxim.

"You're making a common mistake," he said. "You're thinking of failure as the enemy of success. But it isn't at all. Failure is a teacher—a harsh one, perhaps, but the best. You say you have a desk full of rejected manuscripts? That's great! Every one of those manuscripts was rejected for a reason. Have you pulled them to pieces looking for that reason? That's what I have to do when an idea backfires or a sales program fails. You've got to put failure to work for you."

He folded his napkin and put it beside his plate. "You can be discouraged by failure—or you can learn from it. So go ahead and make mistakes. Make all you can. Because, remember, that's where you'll find success. On the far side of failure."

I did remember. My desk was still full of unsalable manuscripts. And when I presented my grand design for a Latin American magazine to the boss, he said acidly, "Do you think we have money to put into a crazy scheme like this? Stop bothering me." (Actually, it wasn't such a bad idea. A year or two later *Reader's Digest* started its Spanish and Portuguese editions, which today are the most widely circulated magazines in Latin America.)

But that's not the point. The point is that somewhere inside me a basic attitude had shifted. A project turned down, a lot of rejected manuscripts—why, these were nothing to be ashamed of. They were rungs in a ladder—that was all. A wise and tolerant man had given me an idea. A simple idea, but a powerful one: If you can learn to learn from failure, you'll go pretty much where you want to go.

The Roadblock of Regret

Nothing in life is more exciting and rewarding than the sudden flash of insight that leaves you a changed person —not only changed, but changed for the better. Such moments are rare, certainly, but they come to all of us. Sometimes from a book, a sermon, a line of poetry. Sometimes from a friend . . . .

That wintry afternoon in Manhattan, waiting in the little French restaurant, I was feeling frustrated and depressed. Because of several miscalculations on my part, a project of considerable importance in my life had fallen through. Even the prospect of seeing a dear friend (the Old Man, as I privately and affectionately thought of him) failed to cheer me as it usually did. I sat there frowning at the checkered tablecloth, chewing the bitter cud of hindsight.

He came across the street, finally, muffled in his ancient overcoat, shapeless felt hat pulled down over his bald head, looking more like an energetic gnome than an eminent psychiatrist. His offices were nearby; I knew he had just left his last patient of the day. He was close to eighty, but he still carried a full case load, still acted as director of a large foundation, still loved to escape to the golf course whenever he could.

By the time he came over and sat beside me, the waiter had brought his invariable bottle of ale. I had not seen him for several months, but he seemed as indestructible as ever.

"Well, young man," he said without preliminary, "what's troubling you?"

I had long since ceased to be surprised at his perceptiveness. So I proceeded to tell him, at some length, just what was bothering me. With a kind of melancholy pride, I tried to be very honest. I blamed no one else for my disappointment, only myself. I analyzed the whole thing, all the bad judgments, the false moves. I went on for perhaps fifteen minutes, while the Old Man sipped his ale in silence.

When I finished, he put down his glass. "Come on," he said. "Let's go back to my office."

"Your office? Did you forget something?"

"No," he said mildly. "I want your reaction to something. That's all."

A chill rain was beginning to fall outside, but his office was warm and comfortable and familiar: book-lined walls, long leather couch, signed photograph of Sigmund Freud, tape recorder by the window. His secretary had gone home. We were alone.

The Old Man took a tape from a flat cardboard box and fitted it onto the machine. "On this tape," he said, "are three short recordings made by three persons who came to me for help. They are not identified, of course. I want you to listen to the recordings and see if you can pick out the two-word phrase that is the common denominator in all three cases." He smiled. "Don't look so puzzled. I have my reasons."

What the owners of the voices on the tape had in common, it seemed to me, was unhappiness. The man who spoke first evidently had suffered some kind of business loss or failure; he berated himself for not having worked harder, for not having looked ahead. The woman who spoke next had never married because of a sense of obligation to her widowed mother; she recalled bitterly all the marital chances she had let go by. The third voice belonged to a mother whose teen-age son was in trouble with the police; she blamed herself endlessly.

The Old Man switched off the machine and leaned back in his chair. "Six times in those recordings a phrase is used that's full of a subtle poison. Did you spot it? No? Well, perhaps that's because you used it three times yourself down in the restaurant a little while ago." He picked up the box that had held the tape and tossed it over to me. "There they are, right on the label. The two saddest words in any language."

I looked down. Printed neatly in red ink were the words: IF ONLY.

"You'd be amazed," said the Old Man, "if you knew how many thousands of times I've sat in this chair and listened to woeful sentences beginning with those two words. '*If only*,' they say to me, 'I had done it differently—or not done it at all. *If only* I hadn't lost my temper, said that cruel thing, made that dishonest move, told that foolish lie. *If only* I had been wiser, or more unselfish, or more self-controlled.' They go on and on until I stop them. Sometimes I make them listen to the recordings you just heard. '*If only*,' I say to them, 'you'd stop saying *if only*, we might begin to get somewhere!' "

The Old Man stretched out his legs. "The trouble with *if only*," he said, "is that it doesn't change anything. It keeps the person facing the wrong way—backward instead of forward. It wastes time. In the end, if you let it become a habit, it can become a real roadblock—an excuse for not trying anymore.

"Now take your own case: Your plans didn't work out. Why? Because you made certain mistakes. Well, that's all right: Everyone makes mistakes. Mistakes are what we learn from. But when you were telling me about them, lamenting this, regretting that, you weren't really learning from them."

"How do you know?" I said, a bit defensively.

"Because," said the Old Man, "you never got out of the past tense. Not once did you mention the future. And in a way—be honest, now!—you were enjoying it. There's a perverse streak in all of us that makes us like to hash over old mistakes. After all, when you relate the story of some disaster or disappointment that has happened to you, you're still the chief character, still in the center of the stage."

I shook my head ruefully. "Well, what's the remedy?"

"Shift the focus," said the Old Man promptly. "Change the key words and substitute a phrase that supplies lift instead of creating drag."

"Do you have such a phrase to recommend?"

"Certainly. Strike out the words 'if only'; substitute the phrase *next time*."

"*Next time?*"

"That's right. I've seen it work minor miracles right here in this room. As long as a patient keeps saying *if only* to me, he's in trouble. But when he looks me in the eye and says *next time,* I know he's on his way to overcoming his problem. It means he has decided to apply the lessons he has learned from his experience, however grim or painful it may have been. It means he's going to push aside the roadblock of regret, move forward, take action, resume living. Try it yourself. You'll see."

My old friend stopped speaking. Outside, I could hear the rain whispering against the windowpane. I tried sliding one phrase out of my mind and replacing it with the other. It was fanciful, of course, but I could hear the new words lock into place with an audible click.

"One last thing," the Old Man said. "Apply this little trick to things that can still be remedied." From the bookcase behind him he pulled out something that looked like a diary. "Here's a journal kept a generation ago by a woman who was a schoolteacher in my hometown. Her husband was a kind of amiable ne'er-do-well, charming but totally inadequate as a provider. This woman had to raise the children, pay the bills, keep the family together. Her diary is full of angry references to Jonathan's weaknesses, Jonathan's shortcomings, Jonathan's inadequacies.

"Then Jonathan died, and all the entries ceased except for one—years later. Here it is: *Today I was made superintendent of schools, and I suppose I should be very proud. But if I knew that Jonathan was out there somewhere beyond the stars, and if I knew how to manage it, I would go to him tonight.*"

The Old Man closed the book gently. "You see? What she's saying is, *if only; if only I had accepted him, faults and all; if only I had loved him while I could.*" He put the book back on the shelf. "That's when those sad words are the saddest of all: when it's too late to retrieve anything."

He stood up a bit stiffly. "Well, class dismissed. It has been good to see you, young man. Always is. Now, if you will help me find a taxi, I probably should be getting on home."

We came out of the building into the rainy night. I spotted a cruising cab and ran toward it, but another pedestrian was quicker.

"My, my," said the Old Man slyly. "If only we had come down ten seconds sooner, we'd have caught that cab, wouldn't we?"

I laughed and picked up the cue. "Next time I'll run faster."

"That's it," cried the Old Man, pulling his absurd hat down around his ears. "That's it exactly!"

Another taxi slowed. I opened the door for him. He

smiled and waved as it moved away. I never saw him again. A month later, he died of a sudden heart attack, in full stride, so to speak.

More than a year has passed since that rainy afternoon in Manhattan. But to this day, whenever I find myself thinking *if only*, I change it to *next time*. Then I wait for that almost-perceptible mental click. And when I hear it, I think of the Old Man.

A small fragment of immortality, to be sure. But it's the kind he would have wanted.

3

The Gift
of Self-Discovery

At times it seems that each of us is condemned to go through life handcuffed to a stranger: ourselves. Who is this peculiar character who shares every moment with us? Why does he (or she) behave the way he (or she) does? Why all these false moves and blunders? Why these irrational likes and dislikes? Why these moods and impulses so unpredictable and so hard to understand?

There are no simple answers: full self-understanding always eludes us. But now and then come unexpected moments of insight or revelation that *seem* to tell us something about ourselves—and in the process something about other people.

I wonder sometimes if the physical setting or background may not be an important factor where these moments of self-discovery are concerned. Certainly in my own case many of them have happened close to the sea. For others I'm sure the background might be the mountains, or even the desert. The main thing is to be in surroundings where strong, environmental forces prevail. I've also noticed that such moments rarely happen when you're feeling altogether happy and contented. They seem to come when you're discouraged, or upset, or at least introspective.

The law of compensation?

Maybe so.

The Turn of the Tide

Not long ago I came to one of those bleak periods that many of us encounter from time to time, a sudden drastic dip in the graph of living when everything goes stale and flat, energy wanes, enthusiasm dies. The effect on my work was frightening. Every morning I would clench my teeth and mutter: "Today life will take on some of its old meaning. You've got to break through this thing. You've got to!"

But the barren days went by, and the paralysis grew worse. The time came when I knew I had to have help.

The man I turned to was a doctor. Not a psychiatrist, just a doctor. He was older than I, and beneath his surface gruffness lay great wisdom and compassion. "I don't know what's wrong," I told him miserably. "I just seem to have come to a dead end. Can you help me?"

"I don't know," he said slowly. He made a tent of his fingers, and gazed at me thoughtfully for a long while. Then, abruptly, he asked, "Where were you happiest as a child?"

"As a child?" I echoed. "Why, at the beach, I suppose. We had a summer cottage there. We all loved it."

"Are you capable of following instructions for a single day?"

"I think so," I said, ready to try anything.

"All right. Here's what I want you to do."

He told me to drive to the beach alone the following morning, arriving not later than nine o'clock. I could take some lunch, but I was not to read, write, listen to the radio, or talk to anyone. "In addition," he said, "I'll give you a prescription to be taken every three hours."

He tore off four prescription blanks, wrote a few words on each, folded them, numbered them and handed them to me. "Take these at nine, twelve, three and six."

"Are you serious?"

He gave a short bark of a laugh. "You won't think I'm joking when you get my bill!"

The next morning, with little faith, I drove to the beach. It was lonely, all right. A northeaster was blowing; the sea looked gray and angry. I sat in the car, the whole day stretching emptily before me. Then I took out the first of the folded strips of paper. On it was written: LISTEN CAREFULLY.

I stared at the two words. Why, I thought, the man must be mad. He had ruled out music and newscasts and human conversation. What else was there?

I raised my head and I did listen. There were no sounds but the steady roar of the sea, the creaking cry of a gull, the drone of some aircraft high overhead. When I got out of the car, a gust of wind slammed the door with a sudden clap of sound. Am I supposed, I asked myself, to listen carefully to things like that?

I climbed a dune and looked out over the deserted beach. Here the sea bellowed so loudly that all other sounds were lost. And yet, I thought suddenly, there must be sounds beneath sounds—the soft rasp of drifting sand, the tiny wind-whisperings in the dune grasses—if the listener got close enough to hear them.

On an impulse I ducked down and, feeling faintly ridiculous, thrust my head into a clump of sea oats. Here I made a discovery: If you listen intently, there is a fractional moment in which everything seems to pause. In that instant of stillness, the racing thoughts halt. For a moment, when you truly listen for something outside yourself, you have to silence the clamorous voices within. The mind rests.

I went back to the car and slid behind the wheel. LISTEN CAREFULLY. As I listened again to the deep growl of the sea, I found myself thinking about the immensity of it, the stupendous rhythms of it, the velvet trap it made for the moonlight, the white-fanged fury of its storms.

I thought of the lessons it had taught us as children. A certain amount of patience (you can't hurry the tides). A great deal of respect (the sea does not suffer fools gladly). An awareness of the vast and mysterious interdependence of things (wind and tide and current, calm and squall and hurricane, all combining to determine the paths of the birds above and the fish below). And the cleanness of it all, with every beach swept twice a day by the great broom of the sea.

Sitting there, I realized I was thinking of things bigger than myself—and there was relief in that.

Even so, the morning passed slowly. The habit of hurling myself at a problem was so strong that I felt lost without it. Once, when I was wistfully eyeing the car radio, a phrase from Carlyle jumped into my head:

> Silence is the element in which great things fashion themselves.

By noon the wind had polished the clouds out of the sky, and the sea had a hard, merry sparkle. I unfolded the second "prescription." And again I sat there, half-amused and half-exasperated. Three words this time: TRY REACHING BACK.

Back to what? To the past, obviously. But why, when all my worries concerned the present or the future?

I left the car and started tramping along the dunes. The doctor had sent me to the beach because it was a place of happy memories. Maybe *that* was what I was supposed to reach for: the wealth of happiness that lay half-forgotten behind me.

I found a sheltered place and lay down on the sun-warmed sand. When I tried to peer into the well of the past, the recollections that came to the surface were happy but not very clear. So I decided to experiment: to work on these vague impressions as a painter would, retouching the colors, strengthening the outlines. I would choose specific incidents and recapture as many details as possible. I would visualize people complete with dress and gestures. I would listen (carefully!) for the exact sound of their voices, the echo of their laughter.

The tide was ebbing now, but there was still thunder in the surf. So I chose to go back across the years to the last fishing trip I made with my younger brother, who died in the Pacific during World War II. I found that if I closed my eyes and really tried I could see him with amazing vividness, even the humor and eagerness in his eyes that far-off morning.

In fact, I could see it all: the ivory scimitar of beach where we were fishing, the eastern sky smeared with sunrise, the great rollers creaming in, stately and slow. I could feel the backwash swirl warm around my knees, see the sudden arc of my brother's rod as he struck a fish, hear his exultant yell. Piece by piece I rebuilt it, clear and unchanged under the transparent varnish of time. Then it was gone.

I sat up slowly. TRY REACHING BACK. Happy people were usually assured, confident people. If, then, you deliberately reached back and touched happiness, might there not be released little flashes of power, tiny sources of strength?

This second period of the day went more quickly. As the sun began its long slant down the sky, my mind ranged eagerly through the past, reliving some episodes, uncovering others that had been almost forgotten. For example, when I was around thirteen and my brother ten, Father had promised to take us to the circus. But at lunchtime there was a phone call; some urgent business required his attention downtown. We braced ourselves for disappointment. Then we heard him say, "No, I won't be down. It'll have to wait."

When he came back to the table, Mother smiled. "The circus keeps coming back, you know."

"I know," said Father. "But childhood doesn't."

Across all the years I remembered this, and knew from the sudden glow of warmth that no kindness is ever really wasted, or ever completely lost.

By three o'clock the tide was out; the sound of the waves was only a rhythmic whisper, like a giant breathing. I stayed in my sandy nest, feeling relaxed and content—and a little complacent. *The doctor's prescriptions,* I thought, *were easy to take.*

But I was not prepared for the next one. This time the three words were not a gentle suggestion. They sounded more like a command. REEXAMINE YOUR MOTIVES.

My first reaction was defensive. *There's nothing wrong with my motives,* I said to myself. *I want to be successful—who doesn't? I want a certain amount of recognition—but so does everybody. I want more security than I've got—and why not?*

"Maybe," said a small voice, "those motives aren't good enough. Maybe that's the reason the wheels have stopped going round."

I picked up a handful of sand and let it stream between my fingers. In the past, whenever my work went well, there had always been something spontaneous about it, something uncontrived, something free. Lately it had been calculated, competent—and dead. Why? Because I had been looking past the job itself to the rewards I hoped it would bring. The work had ceased to be an end in itself; it had become merely a means to make money, pay bills. The sense of giving something, of helping people, of making a contribution, had been lost in a frantic clutch at security.

In a flash of certainty, I saw that if one's motives are wrong, nothing can be right. It makes no difference whether you are a mailman, a hairdresser, an insurance salesman, a housewife—whatever. As long as you feel you are serving others, you do the job well. When you are concerned only with helping yourself, you do it less well—a law as inexorable as gravity.

For a long time I sat there. Far out on the bar I heard the murmur of the surf change to a hollow roar as the tide turned. Behind me the spears of light were almost horizontal. My time at the beach had almost run out, and I felt a grudging admiration for the doctor and the "prescriptions" he had so casually and cunningly devised. I saw, now, that in them was a therapeutic progression that might well be of value to anyone facing any difficulty.

LISTEN CAREFULLY: To calm the frantic mind, slow it down, shift the focus from inner problems to outer things.

TRY REACHING BACK: Since the human mind can hold but one idea at a time, you blot out present worries when you touch the happinesses of the past.

REEXAMINE YOUR MOTIVES: This was the hard core of the so-called treatment—this challenge to reappraise, to bring one's motives into alignment with one's capabilities and conscience. But the mind must be clear and receptive to do this—hence the six hours of quiet that went before.

The western sky was a blaze of crimson as I took out the last slip of paper. Six words this time. I walked slowly out on the beach. A few yards below high-water mark I stopped and read the words again: WRITE YOUR WORRIES ON THE SAND.

I let the paper blow away, reached down and picked up a fragment of shell. Kneeling there under the vault of the sky, I wrote several words, one above the other.

Then I walked away, and I did not look back. I had written my troubles on the sand. The tide was coming in.

The Way of Acceptance

A few years ago, some friends of ours were given the heartbreaking news that their teen-age son was going blind, that nothing could be done. Everyone was torn with pity for them, but they remained calm and uncomplaining. One night, as we left their house, I tried to express my admiration for their fortitude.

I remember how the boy's father looked up at the stars. "Well," he said, "it seems to me that we have three choices. We can curse life for doing this to us, and look for some way to express our grief and rage. Or we can grit our teeth and endure it. Or we can accept it. The first alternative is useless. The second is sterile and exhausting. The third is the only way."

The way of acceptance. How often that path is rejected by people who refuse to admit limitations, who hide behind denials and excuses, who react to trouble with resentment and bitterness. And how often, conversely, when one makes the first painful move toward repairing a damaged relationship, or even a broken life, that move involves acceptance of some thorny and difficult reality that must be faced before the rebuilding can begin.

It's a law that seems to run like a shining thread through the whole vast tapestry of life. Take alcoholism, for instance—that grim and mysterious disease. Where does recovery begin? It begins with acceptance of the unacceptable, with the uncompromising four words with which members of Alcoholics Anonymous introduce themselves at meetings: "I am an alcoholic."

Or take a failing marriage—a marriage that is on the rocks, or drifting toward them. Any marriage counselor will tell you that no reconciliation ever succeeds unless it involves acceptance of the other partner, faults and all, as a fallible, imperfect human being. And acceptance, too, of the fact that the blame for the trouble must be shared.

Difficult? It's hideously difficult. But in terms of courage and cheerfulness and ultimate happiness, the rewards can be beyond measure. I knew a man once, an Episcopal minister, who through some hereditary affliction was deaf and almost blind. He went right on preaching, visiting the sick, listening to people with his hearing aid, laughing uproariously at jokes, giving away huge portions of himself and having a marvelous time.

One Christmas I went with him to buy some trifle in a crowded drugstore. On the back of the entrance door was a mirror, so placed that as we turned to leave, my friend's reflection came forward to meet him. Thinking that someone else was approaching, he stepped aside. So, naturally, did the image. He moved forward and once more met himself. Again he retreated.

By now an uneasy hush had fallen on the spectators. No one quite knew what to say or do. But on his third advance my companion realized that he was facing a mirror. "Why," he cried, "it's only me!" He made a grand bow. "Good to see you, old boy! Merry Christmas!" The whole store exploded in delighted laughter, and I heard someone murmur, "That man really has what it takes." What "it" was, surely, was the gift of acceptance—acceptance of limitations that in turn brought the power to transcend them.

Is there any way to be receptive to this gift, to learn to rebound from the inevitable slings and arrows that wound the ego and try the soul? One way is to face your difficulty, your problem, your loss, to look at it unflinchingly, and then to add two unconquerable words: *and yet*.

Last summer in California, I met a man who had been a skydiver until, on his nineteenth jump, his parachute failed to open fully and his emergency chute wrapped itself around the partially collapsed main chute. He slammed into a dry lake bed at sixty miles an hour. Doctors thought this broken remnant of a man would never leave his hospital bed. They told him so, and he sank into black despair.

But in the hospital he had frequent visits from another patient, a man whose spinal cord had been severed in an automobile accident. This man would never walk, would never, in fact, move a finger again. But he was always cheerful. "I certainly don't recommend my situation to anyone," he would say. "And yet I can read, I can listen to music, I can talk to people . . . ."

And yet: those two words shift the focus from what has been lost to what remains—and to what may still be gained. They gave such hope and determination to the skydiver that he came through his ordeal and today walks without a limp.

Some people confuse acceptance with apathy, but there's all the difference in the world. Apathy fails to distinguish between what can and what cannot be helped; acceptance makes that distinction. Apathy paralyzes the will-to-action; acceptance frees it by relieving it of impossible burdens. Dwight Eisenhower's mother was a deeply religious woman. When the future president was a boy, she would say to him, "Life deals the cards; the way you play them is up to you." There's acceptance in that philosophy—but no hint of apathy.

There was no apathy, either, in the acceptance of our friends whose boy lost his sight. They helped him learn Braille. They convinced him that a life could be useful and happy even though it had to be lived in darkness. He's doing splendidly in college now, and his attitude seems to be a cheerful, "My handicap's blindness. What's yours?"

In such cases, acceptance liberates people by breaking the chains of self-pity. Once you accept the blow, the disappointment, you're free—free to go on to new endeavors that may turn out magnificently.

I remember being given a glimpse of this truth quite early in life. During my first year at college, home for a brief visit, I was faced with the unpleasant necessity of telling my parents that my brave plans for working my way through were not succeeding at all.

The field I had chosen involved selling. Students ran the campus concessions for such things as dry-cleaning and laundry, and freshmen could compete for positions in these organizations by selling service contracts. I waited until my last night at home. Then I told my parents that I had done my best, but that I was not going to be among the successful candidates.

"Why not?" my father asked.

Nothing is so indelible as the memory of failure. I remember how the coal fire muttered in the grate, and the tawny light flickered on the shadowy bookcases. "Because," I said slowly, "I'm a terrible salesman. I get self-conscious and discouraged. Other people do the job much better. I'm in the wrong pew, that's all."

I wait for the remonstrance, the exhortation, the you-can-do-it-if-you-really-try lecture. But the room remained silent. Finally, my father laughed gently. "Well," he said, "that's fine. It's just as important to learn what you can't do as what you can. Now let's forget about that and talk about getting you into the right pew!"

Accept, forget, move on. Some great Americans have ordered their lives along those lines. Abraham Lincoln once told a visitor that in the fiery crucible of the Civil War he did the best he could, regardless of criticism, and would do it to the end. "If the end brings me out all right," he added, "what is said against me won't amount to anything. If the end brings me out wrong, ten angels swearing I was right would make no difference." It was *his* way of describing his acceptance of the frightful responsibility, the awful loneliness of the presidency.

Just as acceptance has its rewards, so nonacceptance has its penalties. We knew a couple once who had three children. The oldest was a girl, sweet-tempered, but very slow. It was clear that there was a degree of mental retardation, but the parents could not bring themselves to accept it. They tried to pretend that the child had normal abilities. They put her in schools where she could not keep up. They begged for performance that she could not give. They tried to rearrange the world to fit her limitations, meanwhile neglecting the emotional needs of their other children. They meant well; they thought they were doing the right thing. But their refusal to accept their child as she really was made life a burden for all of them.

Perhaps in the long run the beginning of wisdom lies in the simple admission that things are not always the way we would like them to be; that we ourselves are not so good or so kind or so hard-working as we would like to believe. And yet—*and yet*—with each sun that rises there is a new day, a new challenge, a new opportunity for doing better.

Oh, Lord, goes one variation of Reinhold Niebuhr's prayer, *grant me the strength to change things that need changing, the courage to accept things that cannot be changed, and the wisdom to know the difference.*

People have called it the prayer of acceptance. They are right.

The Image of Success

One of my most vivid and valuable memories goes back to a mild December afternoon in the Georgia low country where I was born. Vivid because I remember it so clearly. Valuable because, without fully understanding it, I was handed a remarkable bit of wisdom.

A single-barreled, 20-gauge shotgun, given to me for Christmas, had made me the proudest thirteen-year-old in Georgia. On my first hunt, moreover, by a lucky freak I had managed to hit the only bird I got a shot at. My heart almost burst with excitement and pride.

The second hunt was a different story. My companion was an elderly judge, a friend of my father's. He looked rather like a bloodhound, with a seamed brown face and hooded eyes and the easy tolerance that comes from knowing the worst about the human race but liking people just the same. I had some misgivings about hunting with the Judge because I stood in awe of him, and wanted mightily to please him. And I walked straight into humiliation.

We found plenty of birds, and the Judge knocked down one or two on every covey rise. I, on the other hand, didn't touch a feather. I tried everything: shooting over, under, soon, late. Nothing made any difference. And the more I missed, the tenser I got.

Then old Doc, the pointer, spotted a quail in a clump of palmetto. He froze, his long tail rigid. Something in me froze, too, because I knew I was facing one more disgrace.

This time, however, instead of motioning me forward, the Judge placed his gun carefully on the ground. "Let's set a minute," he suggested companionably. Whereupon he took out a pipe and loaded it with blunt fingers. Then, slowly, he said, "Your dad was telling me you hit the first quail you shot at the other day. That right?"

"Yes, sir," I said miserably. "Just luck, I guess."

"Maybe," said the Judge. "But that doesn't matter. Do you remember exactly how it happened? Can you close your eyes and see it all in your mind?"

I nodded, because it was true. I could summon up every detail: the bird exploding from under my feet, the gun seeming to point itself, the surge of elation, the warmth of the praise . . . .

"Well, now," the Judge said easily, "you just sit here and relive that shot a couple of times. Then go over there and kick up that bird. Don't think about me or the dog or anything else. Just think about that one good shot you made the other day—and sort of keep out of your own way."

When I did what he said, it was as if a completely new set of reflexes had come into play. Out flashed the quail. Up went the gun, smoothly and surely, as if it had life and purpose of its own. Seconds later, Doc was at my knee, offering the bird.

I was all for pressing on, but the Judge unloaded his gun. "That's all for today, son," he said. "You've been focusing on failure all afternoon. I want to leave you looking at the image of success."

There, complete in two sentences, was the best advice I'd ever had, or ever would have. Did I recognize it, seize upon it eagerly, act upon it fully? Of course not. I was just a child, delighted with a remarkable trick that somehow worked. I had no inkling of the tremendous psychological dynamics involved.

For a long time, with a child's faith in magic, I used the Judge's advice as a kind of hunting good-luck charm. Later I found that the charm worked in other sports, too. In tennis, say, if at some crucial point you needed a service ace, it was uncanny how often your racket would deliver if you made yourself recall—vividly and distinctly—a previous ace that you had hammered past an opponent.

I know now why this is so. The human organism is a superb machine, engineered to solve fantastic problems. It is perfectly capable of blasting a tennis ball 70 feet onto an area the size of a handkerchief, or putting an ounce of shot traveling more than 100 feet per second exactly where it will intersect the path of a target moving 50 miles an hour. It can do far more difficult things than these—but only if it is not interfered with, if tension does not creep in to stiffen the muscles, dull the reflexes and fog the marvelous computers in the brain.

And tension (which nine times out of ten is based on the memory of past failures), can be reduced or even eliminated by the memory of past success.

At first I applied this image-of-success technique only to athletics. Later I began to see that a similar principle operated for many of the successful career people whom I met through my work. These individuals varied enormously in background, in field of endeavor—even in brains. The one thing they all had in common was confidence.

Once such man, a corporation president, reminisced to me about his first job. "I started my sales career," he said, "by selling pots and pans from door to door. The first day I made only one sale in forty attempts. But I never forgot the face of that woman who finally bought something—how it changed from suspicion and hostility to gradual interest, and final acceptance. For years I used to recall her face as a kind of talisman when the going was rough." To this man, that housewife's face was a mirror which reflected the image of himself as a successful salesman.

There are times when even the brightest talent can be dimmed momentarily if this consciousness of competence is lost. Once I talked with Margaret Mitchell about the frame of mind in which she wrote *Gone with the Wind.* "It was going along pretty well," Miss Mitchell said, "until somebody sent me a new book called *John Brown's Body,* by Stephen Vincent Benet. When I finished reading that magnificent Civil War epic, I burst into tears and put my own manuscript away on a closet shelf. *John Brown's Body* gave me such a terrible case of the humbles that it was months before I could find the necessary faith in myself and my book to go on."

A terrible case of the humbles—what a vivid way of saying that for a while she lost her conviction of competence! And when she lost it, tension took over—and paralyzed her.

The truth is, all of us dread the hurt of failure, even in small things. And it starts young. Children face a world of constantly increasing demands. They need praise and reassurance and the repeated performance of tasks within their powers if the memory of past failures is to be crowded out by the memory of past successes. That was what the wise old judge did for me. When he saw that I was "focusing on failure," he made me turn around and stare at success.

Employing this stratagem is not just wishful thinking. The essence of the magic, it seems to me, is that you visualize something that actually did occur—and therefore can occur again. You brace yourself on a specific, concrete episode in which you functioned well.

Such episodes happen to all of us. Initial failure, to be sure, is the price you pay for learning anything new. The first few times you try to water-ski, you may well topple in a heap. The first few times you try to make a speech or bake a cake, the results may leave much to be desired. But if you keep at it, sooner or later, by luck or the blessed law of averages, there will be a success.

This, then, is the image to fasten on the next time you approach the same problem. Nail it up in your mind like a horseshoe, and it will bring you something better than mere good luck.

The Secret of Self-Renewal

Not long ago I found myself with a group of scientists who were talking about new developments that are radically changing our world. A communications specialist told of laboratory experiments indicating that 200 television programs can be transmitted simultaneously over a cable twice the thickness of a human hair. A physicist described the use of lasers—concentrated light beams—in medicine; a damaged retina in the human eye, he said, can be tacked back into place with these amazing shafts of light. The recital of man's incredible ability to uncover hidden potentials in material things went on and on. Not once did anyone mention the problem of unlocking the latent power in man himself.

Yet, surely, this is the greatest challenge of all! Vast untapped sources of energy exist in every one of us. Now and then, by luck or chance, we make contact with these mysterious reservoirs. We feel a tremendous surge of confidence, creativity, well-being. Then, abruptly, the circuit is broken and we're our old humdrum selves again.

But there are a few individuals for whom the circuit seems to stay open permanently. Such people are more vital, dynamic, productive and alive than the rest of us. They seldom grow weary. They're almost never discouraged. Somehow, they have discovered the secret of self-renewal.

Thinking about this after my meeting with the scientists,

I reviewed the names of friends who seemed especially to belong in this category: a minister in Manhattan, an insurance executive in Chicago, a psychiatrist in Colorado, and a widowed lady in my own hometown. I decided to visit these four people and ask if they had any clues to this secret of self-renewal.

In Manhattan, my clergyman friend sat in his study, and looked at me thoughtfully. "Self-renewal? Well, in a way, that's what religion is all about. You're talking about psychic energy—the quality that underlies zest, eagerness, dynamism—even morality."

"Morality?"

"Definitely. When people are behaving badly, when they're making a mess of things, often it's because they just don't have the strength to cope with their problems. They're not so much evil as enervated; not so much wicked as weary."

"Do you have an answer?"

He smiled. "I'm always suspicious of too-pat answers. But the advice I sometimes offer is this: *Give in to goodness now and then*. I don't mean masochistic self-sacrifice. I mean the deliberate performance of an act that has ethical value: helping someone in need, righting a wrong, forgiving an enemy. For best results, the act should be one that can't possibly benefit you."

"This leads to self-renewal?"

"Why not? Since we live in an ethical universe, the performance of ethical acts must align us with the forces that sustain it. So, if we give in to goodness once in a while, we gain strength. If we consistently refuse, we're at cross-purposes with everything, including our deepest nature. People not only have the capacity for ethical behavior, they have a built-in need for it. If you give in to goodness reasonably often, you won't have to seek self-renewal. It will come to you."

Across from me in a Chicago restaurant sat the insurance executive, gray-haired, calm, and confident. "A formula for self-renewal?" he repeated. "Just four words: EXPOSE YOURSELF TO ENTHUSIASM!"

From his wallet he took a worn newspaper clipping. "I read these words to my salesmen, sometimes: 'No person who is enthusiastic about his work has anything to fear from life. All the opportunities in the world are waiting to be grasped by people who are in love with what they're doing.' "

"Who said it?"

"An American philosopher named Sam Goldwyn. Emerson said it, too: 'Nothing great was ever achieved without enthusiasm.' They're right, you know. Enthusiasm *is* the magic quality. It overcomes inertia, banishes discouragement, gets things done. And the remarkable thing about it is that it's contagious. I found this out when I was just a youngster selling insurance policies door-to-door. Sometimes I'd make fifty calls without a sale, and when I'd get home at night my enthusiasm would be pretty low.

"But in the boardinghouse where I lived there were three old-timers. One ardently collected stamps. Another was a rabid baseball fan. The third hated the mayor of Chicago. I forget why, but he just loved hating the mayor of Chicago. And I found that if I talked to them about their particular interests, they would get so incandescent that their enthusiasm flowed into me, and I got all excited about selling insurance again."

He leaned forward and tapped the table earnestly. "Enthusiasm is the state of caring—*really caring*—about something. Always look for it in others. When you find it, strike sparks from it. Some of those sparks will kindle a fire in you!"

In Denver, the old psychiatrist regarded me with wise and tolerant eyes. "Of course, there are hidden powers in people," he said. "In moments of emergency, tremendous physical energies are often released; a man lifts a wrecked car to free a trapped driver, a woman swims a mile from a capsized boat, towing her child to safety. Such strength comes from the hidden dynamo of the unconscious mind. That's where mental energy comes from, too. By and large, inventive, creative people are those who have managed to keep open the channels between the conscious and unconscious mind."

"But how do you keep the channels open?"

He laughed. "If anyone had the final answer to that, the world would be a very different place. But I have a suggestion: STEP OUT OF YOUR OWN SHADOW."

"What does that mean?"

"It means stop judging yourself so harshly. It means stop focusing on your faults and shortcomings, and give yourself credit for a few virtues now and then. You'd be surprised to know how many people tell me that they're no good, that they're hopeless failures. These people need to be kinder to themselves, because very often self-kindness reduces the feelings of guilt and inferiority that are blocking the flow of power from the unconscious.

"I was talking to a very despondent man just this morning. I said to him, 'Well, sure, you've made some mistakes. Who hasn't? But it seems to me you've beaten yourself over the head long enough. There's a lot ot quiet, unrecognized heroism in people, including you. You say you're selfish. But what percentage of your net income do you actually spend on yourself? Five percent? Ten? The rest goes to your family, doesn't it? How much of your wife's time is spent keeping house and caring for the children? Almost all of it, probably. Remember this: The good in you far outweighs the bad. So be gentle with yourself, and let happiness and self-esteem and energy back into your life!' "

Down in Georgia, where I live, when a lady reaches a certain age and a certain eminence, she begins once more to be called by her first name with a *Miss* in front of it, a title laden with affection, pride, and respect. And often that pride is more than justified, because when you look back at the history of the town and ask yourself who started the symphony or spearheaded the drive for the new hospital or got rid of the courthouse gang, chances are the name that comes to mind will be a feminine one with a Miss in front of it. That's why I went to see Miss Caroline.

"Good heavens, child," said Miss Caroline briskly when I asked her about self-renewal. "It's just the old law of challenge and response, isn't it? When you *meet* a challenge, something in you will respond. It's as simple as that."

"A lot of people don't find it so simple."

"That's because they refuse the challenges. I started out that way myself—afraid to get involved, afraid I might do things wrong, afraid of what people might say if I made mistakes.

"But then the time comes when you see something that needs doing so badly that you're shamed into putting one toe in, and suddenly, miraculously, you find that you do have the energy or persistence or stubbornness or whatever it takes to get the job done.

"This is so exciting, the sense of accomplishment so satisfying, that when the next challenge comes along you accept it. And the magic process starts all over again. A formula for self-renewal? *Find something that needs to be done and start doing it.*"

"Miss Caroline," I said, "I've put that question to four different people in four different parts of the country, and I've had four different answers."

I told her the other answers. She listened thoughtfully. "Well," she said finally, "those answers aren't really so very different. They're all saying the same thing in different ways." She smiled. "I think my grandmother summed it all up in just nine words: LOVE LIFE—AND IT WILL LOVE YOU RIGHT BACK! I've remembered those words ever since I was a little girl, and they cover just about everything. Why don't you settle for that?"

I had to smile, too. "I'll try, Miss Caroline," I said. "I'll surely try."

The Search

It was one of those curiously aimless Sunday afternoons that every family knows. I had driven the children out into the country to look for pinecones and acorns; any objective is better than none! Their mother had a touch of flu; I was mainly interested in letting her get some rest. So we were on our own, the kids and I.

It was one of those hazy autumn days we get sometimes in the Deep South when no wind stirs and the dust motes hang like golden smoke in the soft air. It was also one of those days when I was feeling depressed. No single, overwhelming problem. Just a combination of things. A friend had done me an unkindness, or so I thought. A promising writing assignment had fallen through. There was, inside our family circle, a corrosive little problem of human relationships that stubbornly refused to yield to reason or common sense.

These things kept eddying through my mind, and just about sundown we came across a place that seemed to fit my mood perfectly; a forgotten cemetery in a quiet oak grove, lichen-covered headstones tilted fantastically under a ghostly canopy of Spanish moss. The children ran around like a pack of hounds, making a game of finding the oldest date. ("Hey, look, an 1840!" "Ha, that's young. Here's an 1812!") I stood by one of the weathered stones and watched. Disturbed by the shouts and laughter, a big brown

owl drifted out of a magnolia tree and vanished on reproachful wings. *Don't be upset, old owl,* I said to him in my
mind; *children's voices don't trouble the dead.*

The stone beside me marked the resting place of
somebody's BELOVED WIFE who died in 1865 OF A FEVER.
Beneath her name was a line of script, almost indistinguish-
able. I looked closer, wondering which biblical phrase her
grieving children might have chosen. But it was not a quotation; it was a statement: EVER SHE SOUGHT THE BEST, EVER
FOUND IT.

Eight words. I stood there with my fingers on the cool
stone, feeling the present fade and the past stir behind the
illusion we call time. A century ago this woman had been
living through a hideous war. Perhaps it took her husband
from her, perhaps her sons. When it ended her country was
beaten, broken, impoverished. She must have known
humiliation, tasted despair. Yet someone who knew her
had written that she always looked for the best, and always
found it.

It's strange, sometimes, how a single phrase will haunt
you. As we walked back to the car through the gray twilight,
I could not get this one out of my mind. EVER SHE SOUGHT
THE BEST. There was courage in the words, and dignity, and
purpose. And a kind of triumph, too, as if they contained a
secret of inestimable value. What you look for in life, they
seemed to be saying, you will surely find. But the direction
in which you look is up to you.

The station wagon was waiting by the side of the road. As
the miles fled past, I found myself thinking of the things
that had been bothering me. They were real enough, but
now I saw that I had been focusing, not on the best, but on
the worst. Where my friend was concerned, what was one
misunderstanding compared to years of affection? The lost
assignment was disappointing, but there would be others.

The family difficulty was a rocky little island, but after all, it was surrounded by an ocean of love.

We were home at last. The children straggled in, tired now, ready for their supper. I looked at the house and thought of the worries I had often entertained there like honored guests, inviting them in, spreading banquets before them, giving them a preposterous preference over all the good things the same house contained. *Perhaps,* I told myself, *you've learned something today:* SEARCH FOR THE BEST.

The living room was familiar and quiet; the chair was an old friend; the fire muttered in the grate. *Search for it?* I said to myself. *You don't have to search very far. No one does. It's around us all the time, the goodness, the abundance, the wonder of living. The miracle of it all.*

The five-year-old climbed up on my lap and burrowed his porcupine head into my shoulder. I could see the firelight reflected in his dreaming eyes. "Daddy?"

"Yes?" It would be dark, now, in the old burial ground. Darkness and silence, and the old owl watching the shifting leaf-patterns, and wisdom carved on an ancient stone.

"Tell me a story."

"A story?" *One generation passeth away, and another generation cometh.* "Well, once upon a time . . . ."

4

The Gift of Faith

I remember a cold December afternoon years ago when I was in my early twenties. A friend and I were winding up a day of duck-hunting. We were picking up the decoys when a flight of Canada geese came by. They drove right across the sunset, so low that you could see their wing tips reflected in the burnished water. The sight was so magnificent that I exclaimed, "Look at that! Makes you grateful just to be alive!"

And my friend said quietly, "Grateful to whom?"

That was all he said, but I never forgot those words because they came so close to the cornerstone of my own philosophy —indeed the philosophy that is the theme of this book. The gifts of life, it seems to me, are beyond all counting or all measure. Inevitably they evoke and elicit gratitude. But how can one be grateful for a gift without acknowledging a Giver?

Since that far-off afternoon I have done much reporting in what might be termed the religious field. I have interviewed dozens of people—maybe hundreds—asking questions about their beliefs. Some impressed me more than others, but it is impossible to avoid the conclusion that the gift of faith (and I think it *is* a gift) is the most valuable one of all. People who have it are *stronger*—and *kinder*—and *more unselfish*—and *happier*. It's as simple (and as mysterious) as that.

I will not attempt to say that the stories told me by such people have affected my own beliefs or attitudes in any measurable degree. If a reporter stops being objective he also stops being an accurate reporter, Still, I have often had the feeling that in putting their experiences into words I was passing something along—something of enormous importance—and that perhaps being a transmission belt was what I was designed to be.

Here, then, are some of those experiences as I encountered them along the way.

Act as If

Quite often I've found, in interviewing people, the easiest way to begin is to ask them the question they are best qualified to answer—and the one that most people would like to have answered. As a rule, with luck, all subsequent questions follow easily and naturally.

In this case, the man across the desk was one of America's outstanding clergymen. And so I asked him: "What can a person do to strengthen his religious faith?"

"To tell you the truth," said Dr. Samuel M. Shoemaker, "I get a little tired of people who just sit around wringing their hands and wishing they had more faith. Or *some* faith. Wishing alone won't do it. If you want to learn to ride a bicycle, or swim, or shoot a gun, you don't just sit in your chair and wish, do you? You climb on a bicycle and fall off a few times. You get into the water, even if you're not sure it will hold you up. You find someone who knows how to shoot a gun and try to learn from him."

We were sitting in Dr. Shoemaker's study in the quiet rectory, just the two of us. Outside, sunlight lay like a golden rug on the lawn. Across the street, the spire of Pittsburgh's Calvary Church was sharp against the sky.

"If you want to learn something," Dr. Shoemaker went on in his pleasant Marylander's voice, "you try it. You experiment until you acquire some skill. And that's what you've got to do if you want religion to play a stronger part in your life. You've got to make some spiritual experiments."

"Experiments?" I said. "What sort of experiments?"

Dr. Shoemaker smiled, and I found that already, like most of his congregation, I was thinking of him as Dr. Sam. "Ever hear of the six *X*'s? They make a pretty logical progression, if you list them in order." He ticked the words off his fingers. "They go like this:

> Exposure
> Explanation
> Experiment
> Experience
> Expression
> Expansion

"Now you take the first step: EXPOSURE. Faith is contagious, we all know that. But you've got to come into contact with it to catch it. You've got to make a deliberate decision to expose yourself, to *make* contact. You can't quarantine yourself and expect it to come to you. So the first experiment is really self-exposure."

"What techniques do you recommend?" I asked him. "Going to church? Reading the Bible?"

"Those are obvious ones," said Dr. Sam. "Naturally it helps to go where people talk about God, or to read anything that will focus your attention on His love for us. But I recommend a technique that requires even less effort than that. Just look around you at the people—and there are lots of them, who believe without reservation that God *is,* and that He is love, and that He has power in Himself with which to help baffled, struggling human beings.

"The more you observe them, the more you realize that these people are extraordinary. They meet sorrow and pain with serenity. They're patient with the shortcomings of others. They'll make every effort to help a person in trouble. There's a kind of power in them, but they know very well, and will tell you if you ask them, that the power comes *through* them, not from them. You can't be around them without recognizing the special quality they have. And that makes you envy it. And that may start the process of your own search for it."

"Suppose it does," I said. "Suppose the search begins. Are there any attitudes you must adopt?"

"Certainly," said Dr. Sam. "In the first place, you've got to make a conscious effort to be open to the stream of God's power. There's no use going where it is if you won't let it in. You might as well try to take a shower wearing rubber boots, a raincoat, and a sou'wester. The world is full of buttoned-up people, unfortunately, and a lot of them go to church. But they don't sing hymns, they don't join in the responses. They imprison themselves in a dungeon of self-consciousness.

"Now, people like that often need to get into the stream of God's power. If they want to be participants, and not just spectators, they've got to forget about themselves. The great psychologist, William James, said self-surrender was the turning point in religious experience, and he was right." Dr. Sam grinned suddenly. "He was also the one who said that religion is either a dull habit or an acute fever."

I said I hadn't realized William James wrote such lively prose.

"Sure he did, sure he did!" cried Dr. Sam. "His brother Henry, the novelist, he was the dull one! But let's get back to our experiments. I was saying that you've got to open yourself to the stream of God's power. To do that, you've got to believe that it can happen to you. If you decide it's all impossible, if you say to yourself, 'Oh, I could never have anything like that!' you're blocking the flow of power as definitely as when you shut off a stream of water by twisting the tap. You've got to keep reminding yourself that God wants you in contact with Himself. He made you for this very purpose. If not, what *are* you doing here? And He'll help you, if you really search for Him, and hope and pray and try to believe."

"Isn't it hard to pray," I said, "if you're not sure what you're praying to?"

"That doesn't matter," said Dr. Sam firmly. "Give as much of yourself as you can to as much of God as you can understand. You may be a selfish materialist coming to a God who seems impossibly vague. No matter. Come honestly, as you are. Horace Bushnell once said, 'Pray to the dim God, confessing the dimness for honesty's sake.'"

"But how do you know when you're in touch?"

"Sometimes you don't. If you're honest with yourself, you will admit this. But you've got to be honest with God, too. Why not try saying *to* Him whatever you may feel like saying about Him? If, for instance, you doubt that He exists, tell Him so, and tell Him why. That may sound ridiculous, but it's not. And when you're through telling Him, stop and listen. Maybe you'll hear something."

"What if you don't?"

"Well, you've got to keep trying, that's all. You won't necessarily hear, or get, exactly what you want, you know. Jerome Ellison once said he thought that human disbelief is partly pique and exasperation that God won't behave the way we want Him to. We all have to watch this tendency to be demanding in our prayers. There have been times in my own when I could almost imagine the Lord saying, 'Now, wait a minute—which of us is God anyway?'"

I looked at my watch. I had promised not to take up too much of Dr. Sam's time. "We've been talking about things you should do," I said. "Are there also things you should avoid, things that act as deterrents, or set up blocks?"

"Of course there are," said Dr. Sam. "Some of the blocks may be outside yourself. You meet people whose approach to religion seems to be mainly superstitious. Or even downright hysterical. That doesn't help. Or you attend church where the minister tries to explain everything before his listeners have had a chance to formulate their questions, with the result that his audience becomes confused, or bored, or both.

"But the main blocks are likely to be in yourself. Anger, hatred, jealousy, resentment of other people. Fear and guilt. You've got to surrender those little luxuries. And of course, when you make a sincere effort to do that, you find you can't let go of them without letting go of yourself. Self-surrender turns out to be the key, just as William James said. You can't get rid of your sins without getting rid of yourself. That's what Christ meant by being born again."

I observed that a good many people seemed somewhat confused as to what sin was.

Dr. Sam laughed. "There are plenty of definitions. I heard a good one the other day from a young minister. He said that sin was the refusal to be loved by God. That covers a lot of ground, and the more you think about it, the truer it seems. Someone else said that love was the power to communicate. So if you won't let God love you, you're not in touch with Him."

It was quiet in the room for a moment. Then Dr. Sam went on. "I do think," he said, "that most people tend to think of sin in terms of big, black, specific transgression. But complacency and selfishness and unwillingness to admit God into our lives are just as damaging, and far more common. Indifference—the conviction that we get along without God—that's probably the most universal modern sin. And it stems from the oldest and deepest sin of all: *pride.*"

"There's something appealing about some sinners," I said. "They're—well, they're just so human." And I told him about the well-known movie star who had remarked, after a thoroughly misspent life, that his only regret was that his net income had never quite kept up with his gross habits.

Dr. Sam threw back his head and laughed. "Oh," he said, "that's wonderful!"

He moved over to the window and stared out for a moment at the placid afternoon. Then he turned around. "I think I know what lies behind your question," he said. "The people you're talking about are looking for more than just a belief that God exists; they're looking for the certainty of Him in their own lives and experience. Well, there isn't any pat formula that will fit all cases. Religion would be a pretty dull thing if there were. But I'm sure of this: God's interest in us is a lot more steadfast and trustworthy than our interest in Him. He'll get through to us if we give Him any sort of chance. And the channel He uses is precisely the thing we're talking about: *faith.* All of us have the capacity for it. But we have to *use* it.

"I think it's possible to be too self-conscious about our faith, or lack of it. Jesus didn't spend much time analyzing the difficulty of faith for people. He began with faith as an axiom. At times He seemed to be ignoring theology, and even ethics, and urging His listeners just to have faith and trust in the goodness of God—to go for that and everything would turn out for the best. At least . . ." Dr. Sam rubbed his chin ruefully, "that's the way it seems to me. Am I being any help at all?"

I nodded, wondering if my memory would retain even half of the helpful things he had said.

He came back from the window and sat down again. "I've

enjoyed this talk," he said. "But don't rely too much on words, or ideas. You'll find the best reflection of religion in people's lives, not in statements or discussions. Ideas are nebulous to some people, and words sometimes invite arguments. But life—well, stay with it, watch for faith in action, and you'll see concrete examples of what I've been talking about. You'll see more than theory; you'll see proof that it works."

"You've mentioned several specific things," I said, "that a person can do to strengthen his faith. Is there any generalized advice, spiritual or otherwise, that you'd like me to pass along to the doubters and the groping ones?"

Dr. Sam hesitated. "Well," he said finally, "the advice I often give to such people is simply this: *act as if.* Act as if the whole thing, the Gospel, the Good News, the reality and love of God as revealed by Christ—act as if it were all true. Never mind if you have doubts, never mind if you feel it's all too good to be true. Act as if it were so. Behave as if you believed! This isn't self-deception; it's just another spiritual experiment. And it may well have verifiable results.

"Tell the doubters and the shaky ones to try the way of believing as against the way of not believing. If they do try, and stick to it, more and more they'll find themselves being swept along by a current not of their own making. Their level of faith will begin to rise, because the faculty of faith grows stronger with use, and by acting as if they'll have been using it!"

We talked a little while longer, Dr. Sam and I. Then it was time to go. "Well," I said at the front door, "you must keep pretty busy. And you must have a lot of fun."

"Fun?" cried Dr. Sam, wringing my hand. "Fun? We don't have enough buckets around here to catch it all!"

And the great warmth of the man followed me down the street and has followed me since.

The Answer

The day had been long and hot. Some of us had spent most of it struggling with one of those civil rights problems that plague American towns from time to time. It had all been painfully familiar: the mayor listening in troubled silence; the surface politeness masking the deep grievances; the helpless feeling of having left the old simple right-or-wrong far behind and reached the arid region where right clashes endlessly with right.

I came home tired and discouraged. "At times it seems hopeless," I said dejectedly to my wife. "The wounds are too old; the scar tissue is too thick. There just isn't any answer."

She was standing at the kitchen sink making a salad. "Oh, I don't know," she said. "I heard a pretty good answer today. Down at the hospital."

(As a hospital volunteer, my wife pushes a cart full of magazines and paperbacks. She talks to patients, and patients talk to her. Sometimes, bored or lonely, they tell her all sorts of things about themselves.) In this case, she said, the editor of a small country newspaper was convalescing from an operation. She dried her hands on a dish towel.

"You ought to stop by and let him tell you the story he told me. I think you'd be impressed."

"Why can't you tell me what he said?" I asked.

"It wouldn't be the same. You ought to get it from him."

And so the next day I stopped by the hospital. The patient was still there, padding around in a dressing gown and slippers—a tall man with gentle blue eyes and a gift for words. We sat in the visitors' lounge, and this is the story he had to tell . . . .

I was a timid six-year-old with braces on my legs, a frail, lost, lonely little boy when I first arrived at the farm in Georgia. Had it not been for an extraordinary woman, I might have remained that way.

She lived on the farm in a two-room cabin where her parents had been slaves. To an outsider she looked like any of the black people on the place in her shapeless gray dress. But to those who knew her she was a spiritual force whose influence was felt everywhere.

She was the first person called when there was sickness; she made medicines from roots and herbs that seemed to cure just about anything. She had a family of her own, but all of the children around felt that somehow they belonged to her. Her name reflected this. In the soft speech of the Georgia lowlands the word *maum* is a slurred version of *mama*. We called her Maum Jean.

Maum Jean talked to the Lord often and we all suspected that when she did, He stopped whatever He was doing, listened, and took appropriate action. Her heart reached out to small, helpless things, so she took particular interest in me from the start.

When I was stricken with polio at the age of three, I'm sure my parents didn't know what was the matter with me. All they knew was that times were hard and suddenly they had a crippled child on their hands. They took me to a New York City hospital, left me, and never came back. The people who took me into their foster home had relatives on the Georgia estate where I was sent in hopes that the warmer climate might help.

Maum Jean's sensitive emotional antenna instantly picked up the loneliness and withdrawal inside me, just as her marvelous diagnostic sense surveyed the polio damage and decided that, regardless of what the doctors might have said, something more ought to be done. Maum Jean had never heard the word *atrophy*, but she knew that muscles could waste away unless used. And so every night when her tasks were done she would come to my room and kneel beside my bed to massage my legs.

Sometimes, when I would cry out with pain, she would sing old songs or tell me stories. When her treatments were over, she would always talk earnestly to the Lord, explaining that she was doing what she could but that she would need help, and when that day came she wanted Him to give her a sign.

A creek wound through the farm and Maum Jean, who had never heard of hydrotherapy, said there was strength in running water. She made her grandsons carry me down to a sandy bank where I could splash around pretty well.

Slowly I grew taller, but there was little change in my legs. I still used crutches; I still buckled on the clumsy braces. Night after night Maum Jean continued the massaging and praying. Then one morning, when I was about twelve, she told me she had a surprise for me.

She led me out into the yard and placed me with my back against an oak tree; I can feel the rough bark of it to this day. She took away my crutches and braces. She moved back a dozen paces and told me that the Lord had spoken to her in a dream. He had said that the time had come for me to walk. "So now," said Maum Jean, "I want you to walk over here to me."

My instant reaction was fear. I knew I couldn't walk unaided; I had tried. I shrank back against the solid support of the tree. Maum Jean continued to urge me.

I burst into tears. I begged. I pleaded. Her voice rose suddenly, no longer gentle and coaxing but full of power and command. "You can walk, boy! The Lord has spoken! Now walk over here."

She knelt down and held out her arms. And somehow, impelled by something stronger than fear, I took a faltering step, and another, and another, until I reached Maum Jean and fell into her arms, both of us weeping.

It was two more years before I could walk normally, but I never used the crutches again. For a while longer I lived in my twilight world, halfway between the whites, who considered me part alien, and the blacks, who could offer affection but no kinship. Then a circus came through town, and when it left, I left with it.

For the next few years I worked with one circus or another. Now and then, when the circus went into winter quarters, I would come back to the little town and help the editor of the weekly newspaper. There was little money in it, but I liked the smell of ink and the sound of words. I never went back to the farm; a runaway seldom returns. But I always asked about Maum Jean, and when I could afford it I sent her little things.

Then the night came when one of Maum Jean's tall grandsons knocked on my door. It was late; there was frost in the air. Maum Jean was dying, he said; she wanted to see me.

The old cabin was unchanged: floors of cypress, windows with wooden shutters—no glass, roof of palm thatch mixed with pitch. Maum Jean lay in bed surrounded by silent watchers, her frail body covered by a patchwork quilt. From a corner of the room, a kerosene lamp cast a dim saffron light. Her face was in shadow, but I heard her whisper my name. Someone put a chair close to the bed. I sat down and touched her hand.

For a long time I sat there. Around me the dark faces were

grave and patient. There were no tears, no chants, all was quiet. Now and then Maum Jean spoke softly. Her mind was clear. She hoped I remembered the things she had taught me. Outside, the night wind stirred. In the other room the fire snapped, throwing orange sparks. There was a long silence; she lay with her eyes closed. Then the old voice spoke, stronger suddenly. "Oh," said Maum Jean with surprise and gladness, "It's so *beautiful!*" She gave a little contented sigh, and died.

And then something quite unbelievable happened: In the semidarkness her face seemed to glow. No one had touched the lamp. There was no other source of light. But her features, which had been almost invisible, could be seen plainly, and she was smiling. It lasted for perhaps ten seconds. It was most strange, but not at all frightening. I couldn't account for it then, and I can't account for it now. But I saw it. We all saw it. Then it faded and was gone . . . .

My companion stopped speaking. In the corridor I heard the rattle of an instrument cart as a nurse hurried by. Finally he spoke again. "All that happened a long time ago. I live in another town, now. But I still think of Maum Jean often, and the main thing she taught me: that nothing is a barrier when love is strong enough. Not age. Not race. Not anything."

I took a deep breath, remembering what my wife had said. The answer? Maybe someday. Someday . . . .

The Miraculous Staircase

Every now and then a reporter comes across a fact, or a set of facts, for which there is no satisfactory or logical explanation. One way to handle such a paradox is to ignore it. Another—more fun—is to let your imagination try to supply the missing ingredients. Then, of course, you are dealing with myth, or legend, or even fiction. But sometimes legend can be a shimmering cloak for truth.

I came across a hidden story like that one time in Santa Fe. I thought about it for a while, and eventually it turned out like this . . . .

On that cool December morning in 1878, sunlight lay like an amber rug across the dusty streets and adobe houses of Santa Fe. It glinted on the bright tile roof of the almost completed Chapel of Our Lady of Light and on the nearby windows of the convent school run by the Sisters of Loretto. Inside the convent, the Mother Superior looked up from her packing as a tap came on her door.

"It's *another* carpenter, Reverend Mother," said Sister Francis Louise, her round face apologetic. "I told him that you're leaving right away, that you haven't time to see him, but he says . . . ."

"I know what he says," Mother Magdalene said, going on resolutely with her packing. "That he's heard about our problem with the new chapel. That he's the best carpenter in all of New Mexico. That he can build us a staircase to the choir loft despite the fact that the brilliant architect in Paris who drew the plans failed to leave any space for one. And despite the fact that five master carpenters have already tried and failed. You're quite right, Sister; I don't have time to listen to that story again."

"But he seems such a nice man," said Sister Francis Louise wistfully, "and he's out there with his burro, and . . . ."

"I'm sure," said Mother Magdalene with a smile, "that he's a charming man, and that his burro is a charming donkey. But there's sickness down at the Santo Domingo Pueblo, and it may be cholera. Sister Mary Helen and I are the only ones here who've had cholera. So we have to go. And you have to stay and run the school. And that's that!" Then she called, "Manuela!"

A young Indian girl of twelve or thirteen, black-haired and smiling, came in quietly on moccasined feet. She was a mute. She could hear and understand, but the sisters had been unable to teach her to speak. The Mother Superior spoke to her gently: "Take my things down to the wagon, child. I'll be right there." And to Sister Francis Louise: "You'd better tell your carpenter friend to come back in two or three weeks. I'll see him then."

"Two or three weeks! Surely you'll be home for Christmas?"

"If it's the Lord's will, Sister. I hope so."

In the street, beyond the waiting wagon, Mother Magdalene could see the carpenter, a bearded man, strongly built and taller than most Mexicans, with dark eyes and a smiling, windburned face. Beside him, laden with tools and scraps of lumber, a small gray burro stood patiently. Manuela was stroking its nose, glancing shyly at its owner. "You'd better explain," said the Mother Superior, "that the child can hear him, but she can't speak."

Good-byes were quick—the best kind when you leave a

place you love. Southwest, then, along the dusty trail, the mountains purple with shadow, the Rio Grande a ribbon of green far off to the right. The pace was slow, but Mother Magdalene and Sister Mary Helen amused themselves by singing songs and telling Christmas stories as the sun marched up and down the sky. And their leathery driver listened and nodded.

Two days of this brought them to Santo Domingo Pueblo, where the sickness was not cholera after all, but measles, almost as deadly in an Indian village. And so they stayed, helping the harassed Father Sebastian, visiting the dark adobe hovels where feverish brown children tossed and fierce Indian dogs showed their teeth.

At night they were bone-weary, but sometimes Mother Magdalene found time to talk to Father Sebastian about her plans for the dedication of the new chapel. It was to be in April; the archbishop himself would be there. And it might have been dedicated sooner, were it not for this incredible business of a choir loft with no means of access—unless it were a ladder.

"I told the bishop," said Mother Magdalene, "that it would be a mistake to have the plans drawn in Paris. If something went wrong, what could we do? But he wanted our chapel in Santa Fe patterned after the Sainte Chapelle in Paris, and who am I to argue with Bishop Lamy? So the talented Monsieur Mouly designs a beautiful choir loft high up under the rose window, and no way to get to it."

"Perhaps," sighed Father Sebastian, "he had in mind a heavenly choir. The kind with wings."

"It's not funny," said Mother Magdalene a bit sharply. "I've prayed and prayed, but apparently there's no solution at all. There just isn't room on the chapel floor for the supports such a staircase needs."

The days passed, and with each passing day Christmas drew closer. Twice, horsemen on their way from Santa Fe to

Albuquerque brought letters from Sister Francis Louise. All was well at the convent, but Mother Magdalene frowned over certain paragraphs. "The children are getting ready for Christmas," Sister Francis Louise wrote in her first letter. "Our little Manuela and the carpenter have become great friends. It's amazing how much he seems to know about us all . . . ."

And what, thought Mother Magdalene, is the carpenter still doing there?

The second letter also mentioned the carpenter. "Early every morning he comes with another load of lumber, and every night he goes away. When we ask him by what authority he does these things, he smiles and says nothing. We have tried to pay him for his work, but he will accept no pay . . . ."

Work? What work? Mother Magdalene wrinkled up her nose in exasperation. Had that softhearted Sister Francis Louise given the man permission to putter around in the new chapel? With firm and disapproving hand, the Mother Superior wrote a note ordering an end to all such unauthorized activities. She gave it to an Indian pottery-maker on his way to Santa Fe.

But that night the first snow fell, so thick and heavy that the Indian turned back. Next day at noon the sun shone again on a world glittering with diamonds. But Mother Magdalene knew that another snowfall might make it impossible for her to be home for Christmas. By now the sickness at Santo Domingo was subsiding. And so that afternoon they began the long ride back.

The snow did come again, making their slow progress even slower. It was late on Christmas Eve, close to midnight, when the tired horses plodded up to the convent door. But the lamps still burned. Manuela flew down the steps, Sister Francis Louise close behind her. And chilled and weary though she was, Mother Magdalene sensed instantly an excitement, an electricity in the air that she could not understand.

Nor did she understand it when they led her, still in her heavy wraps, down the corridor, into the new, as-yet-unused chapel where a few candles burned. "Look, Reverend Mother," breathed Sister Francis Louise. "Look!"

Like a curl of smoke the staircase rose before them, as insubstantial as a dream. Its base was on the chapel floor; its top rested against the choir loft. Nothing else supported it; it seemed to float on air. There were no banisters. Two complete spirals it made, the polished wood gleaming softly in the candlelight. "Thirty-three steps," whispered Sister Francis Louise. "One for each year in the life of our Lord."

Mother Magdalene moved forward like a woman in a trance. She put her foot on the first step, then the second, then the third. There was not a tremor. She looked down, bewildered, at Manuela's ecstatic, upturned face. "But it's impossible! There wasn't time!"

"He finished yesterday," the sister said. "He didn't come today. No one has seen him anywhere in Santa Fe. He's gone."

"But *who* was he? Don't you even know his *name?*"

The sister shook her head, but now Manuela pushed forward, nodding emphatically. Her mouth opened; she took a deep, shuddering breath; she made a sound that was like a gasp in the stillness. The nuns stared at her, transfixed. She tried again. This time it was a syllable, followed by another. "Jo-sé." She clutched the Mother Superior's arm and repeated the first word she had ever spoken. "José!"

Sister Francis Louise blessed herself. Mother Magdalene felt her heart contract. José—the Spanish word for *Joseph.* Joseph the Carpenter. Joseph the Master Woodworker of . . . .

"José!" Manuela's dark eyes were full of tears. "José!"

Silence, then, in the shadowy chapel. No one moved. Far away across the snow-silvered town Mother Magdalene heard a bell tolling midnight. She came down the stairs and took Manuela's hand. She felt uplifted by a great surge of wonder and gratitude and compassion and love. And she knew what it was. It was the spirit of Christmas. And it was upon them all.

Just a legend? Of course. But all good legends contain a grain of truth, and in this case the irrefutable fact at the heart of the legend is the inexplicable staircase itself.

You may see it yourself in Santa Fe today. It stands just as it stood when the chapel was dedicated almost a century ago—except for the banister, which was added later. Tourists stare and marvel. Architects shake their heads and murmur, "Impossible." No one knows the identity of the designer-builder. All the sisters know is that the problem existed, a stranger came, solved it, and left.

The thirty-three steps make two complete turns without central support. There are no nails in the staircase; only wooden pegs. The curved stringers are put together with exquisite precision, spliced in seven places on the inside and nine on the outside. The wood is said to be a hard-fir variety, nonexistent in New Mexico. School records show that no payment for the staircase was ever made.

Who is real and who is imaginary in this version of the story? Mother Mary Magdalene was indeed the first Mother Superior; she came to Santa Fe by riverboat and covered wagon in 1852. Bishop J. B. Lamy was indeed her bishop. And Monsieur Projectus Mouly of Paris was indeed the absentminded architect.

Sister Francis Louise? Well, there must have been someone like her. And Manuela, the Indian girl, came out of nowhere to help with the embroidery.

The carpenter himself? Ah, who can say?

The Secret

There's a question that you ask them when they're obviously on their way to the absolute top of the tree, and so I asked it. "How'd you get started?" I said. "Who or what provided the necessary push?"

She gave me a quizzical look. She wasn't really pretty, but she had a merry sort of face. "That," she said, "is a stock question. But never mind: I can give you an answer. We'll have to go back about fifteen years, though."

"That's all right," I said. "Do we have time?"

"We have about five minutes," she said. "That'll do."

And, standing there in the chilly dampness, this is what she told me.

In those days, she lived in the twilight land between childhood and adolescence, and she didn't like it much. She was eight years old; she was awkward as a newborn colt, and when she looked in the mirror—which was as seldom as possible—all she could see was a pair of enormous eyes and a lot of complicated bands on her teeth. She was shy, she was lonely, she was convinced that she was hideous. Her name was Margaret, but everyone called her Maggie.

To make matters worse, she had a sister named Sybil who seemed to be everything she was not. Sybil was sixteen, blonde, and cunningly streamlined. She had decided opinions, and on this particular wintry afternoon she was voicing one of them—loudly. "Oh, Mother," she wailed, "do we have to take Maggie? She's only a *child*. And she can't even skate!"

"The Bancrofts asked her, dear," their mother said. "It won't do you any harm to have her along."

Sybil clutched her honey-colored ponytail. "But Larry is taking me! It's all arranged. He . . . ."

"He can take you both," their mother said in tones that even Sybil recognized as final. "Heavens, it's only an afternoon skating party!"

Sybil gave her sister a baleful glance.

"You needn't worry," said Maggie in a small voice. "I'll sit in the backseat and not say a word."

He came at three o'clock, tall, lithe, the best athlete in the high school. He was seventeen, but he seemed older; there was a kind of quiet assurance about him. Sybil explained in tragic tones that they would have a passenger. Larry looked at Maggie and smiled a little. "That's all right," he said.

They went down the snowy path to the street, Sybil on Larry's arm, Maggie stumbling along behind like a lost puppy. Sybil opened the rear door for her sister. Larry raised one dark eyebrow, but said nothing.

They drove to the lake where the Bancrofts lived, a sheet of magnificent black ice under the gray December sky. Already twenty or thirty skaters were swooping and spinning, their cries thin and sweet in the frosty air. On the shore a bonfire blazed. There were hamburgers and gallons of hot chocolate.

Larry laced Sybil's skates for her. He offered to lace the pair that Maggie had been given for Christmas, but she refused. She would just sit on a blanket, she said, and watch. No, thanks; she wasn't hungry.

She sat there, small and alone, feeling her fingers and toes grow numb. Out on the ice the skaters circled like bright birds, their runners making rhythmic whirring sounds. Watching them, she felt a longing that was almost like physical pain, a longing to be as graceful as they were, as beautiful—as free.

Larry must have been watching her, for suddenly he left the ice and came over, walking on the tips of his skates. He looked down at her. "How about giving it a try?"

She shook her head, mute and miserable.

"Why not?" he persisted. "It's fun."

"I'm no good at it."

"So what?" He sounded genuinely surprised.

She stared at her mittened hands. "My father says that anything worth doing is worth doing well."

He did not say anything for a moment. Then he knelt, unlaced his skates, slipped on his moccasins. "Come on—let's go."

She looked up at him, startled. "Go? Go where?"

"Over there behind that point of trees. Bring your skates."

"Oh, no," she said. "I couldn't. Sybil . . . ."

"Never mind Sybil." His hand was under her elbow, strong, insistent. Incredibly, she was on her feet, walking beside him through the silver dusk. She said, feebly, "Don't you like Sybil?"

"Sure," he said. "I like her fine. I like you, too."

Around the point was a little cove, frozen, secluded, quiet. "This will do," he said. "Put on your skates."

"But I . . . ."

"Put them on. I'll lace them for you."

He laced hers, then his own. He stepped lightly onto the ice and held out his hand. "Come on, Maggie."

She shook her head, her eyes full of tears. "I can't. I'm afraid . . . ."

He said, gently, "I'll tell you why you're afraid. You're afraid because you're lonely. I know because I was lonely once, just like you. Afraid to try things. Afraid of not doing things well. Afraid of being laughed at. But finally I found out something."

He came back and stood beside her. She stared up at him, puzzled, questioning. It was so quiet that she could hear her heart beating. Around them the sentinel pines stood black and motionless. Above the pines, now, the first star gleamed.

"It's funny," he said. "I couldn't tell this to Sybil. I didn't think I could tell it to anyone. But I can tell it to you. What I found out was very simple. It's that no one is ever really alone. Even when there's no other person around, there still must be—Someone. Someone who made you and therefore cares what happens to you. Someone who will help you if you do the best you can. So you're never alone. You *can't* be alone, no matter what you do. That's the secret of happiness, of doing things well, of everything." He held out his hand again. "Come on, Maggie."

She got to her feet and stood there, wavering. But now his right arm was around her waist, his left hand held hers. "All right, now; just relax. Slide your left foot forward and push with your right. That's it. Now slide the right and push with your left! Fine! Now once more . . . and again . . . and again . . . ."

That was the story she told me, in five minutes or less. Then the lights went out in the big arena, the music blared, the spotlight caught her as she left me standing in the runway and flashed across the ice on glittering skates to meet the members of the troupe who came spilling out of the other runway. The crowd roared as the rink became a whirling kaleidoscope of color and rhythm and movement. The Greatest Ice Show on Earth, they called it, and I guess it was.

A few yards away I saw her husband standing in the darkness, watching, as he did every night. I moved up and stood beside him. He gave me a quick smile, but all of his attention was out there on the ice. "She's wonderful, isn't she," he said, and it was a statement, not a question.

I looked at his face, so eager and proud. A reporter isn't supposed to feel much, but somewhere inside of me there was a little unaccustomed glow.

"Both of you are, Larry," I said.

But he wasn't even listening.

The Hidden Treasure

For millions of people on this troubled planet the year's most poignant moment is dawn on Easter Sunday. It's easy to see why this should be so. Man's deepest dread is the fear of extinction, of being blown out like a candle, of ceasing to be. But on Easter morning, as sunrise leaps across oceans and plains and mountains, Christians everywhere feel a mighty surge of hope in their hearts and are comforted.

All of us have special Easters to look back on. Once, on an ocean liner, I remember there was a sunrise service. I can see it all still: the first spears of light in the east, the wake arrowing away into the dark, the ageless words of the ageless story.

Afterward the other passengers drifted away, and I found myself at the rail with the chief engineer. He was an old Scotsman, practical and blunt, but with a streak of poetry in him. We had become good friends, as sometimes happens on a sea voyage. The horizon was empty; our ship was alone. But the service left me with a strange, exhilarating sense of companionship—of having been part of something unseen but very powerful. When I mentioned this, the old Scot did not seem surprised.

"Aye," he said, "what you felt was the treasure, no doubt." And as the dawn raced over us, he went on to explain what he meant.

It was a bit fanciful he admitted, and he could not remember where the idea came from—far back in his childhood, perhaps from his old Gaelic nurse—the idea that ever since the first Easter a vast treasure had been accumulating.

Not gold, not silver, not anything like that. No, he said, in this invisible treasure-house were stored all the thoughts, all the emotions that Easter had evoked in countless minds and hearts down through the centuries. All the reverence, the awe and wonder, the love and yearning, the gratitude and prayers.

These things, he said, did not just happen and vanish. Like particles of energy, they had their own permanence; none was ever lost. They were all still *there*—out of sight, certainly; out of time, perhaps—but with an unending reality of their own, a kind of infinite reservoir that could be sensed and drawn upon by human beings.

"And that," he concluded matter-of-factly, knocking out his pipe against the railing, "is what you were feeling just now: the hidden treasure of Easter."

A fanciful thought, indeed, coming from a man who lived and worked with machinery. But after all, is the idea really so farfetched? We're conditioned to think of reality in terms of tangibles, it's true. But deep within us we know that we are not just nerve and sinew, blood and bone, or even the whirling electrons that underlie and sustain such illusions. We are something more. We are hopes and dreams. We are the great paired opposites: joy and pain, anger and tenderness, tears and laughter. Surely, weighed in the ultimate scale, such things count as much as the measurables that surround us.

In any case, I like to think that the old Scotsman was right—that in the legacies of past Easters there is faith to be borrowed, strength to be sought, courage to be found. Each of us has his problems, his areas of weakness, his moments of despair. But still the triumphant cry comes ringing through the ages: *Be of good cheer; I have overcome the world.*

And it will come again this year, when light pours over the rim of the world and once more it is Easter Day.

5

The Gift of Bright Encounters

Life, they say, is full of surprises. And so it is. Some are exciting discoveries. Some are unpleasant shocks. My experience has been that the memory of the shocks fades rather quickly. But some of the pleasant surprises remain vivid for years.

As a rule, when the happy lightning strikes, you're not doing anything out of the ordinary. You may be taking a child to school, or going for a casual meeting with a stranger. You're half-asleep in the humdrum of daily living when suddenly something happens. Abruptly, circumstances arrange themselves so that the commonplace becomes the significant and the routine the memorable—so memorable that perhaps it changes you for the rest of your life.

Sometimes what you encounter is simply a time and a place. I remember one night walking alone through the blackout in London during World War II. There had been an air-raid warning, with searchlights crisscrossing the sky, but now the sirens were sounding the all clear. Suddenly all the searchlights were extinguished except for four, one on each side of the city. These great shafts of light ceased moving and grew still, focused on a single point exactly overhead. I stopped walking. They remained there like silver sword blades quartering the tremendous blue-black vault of midnight. The sirens died away, and there was no other sound. Nothing. Just a deep, ringing silence. It was like being at the heart of a gigantic star sapphire. I never forgot that moment, and I never will.

Usually, though, a truly memorable encounter involves someone else. There has to be an exchange of some kind, an insight, an awareness that lingers in the mind, impervious to time. Afterward you know that you have learned something valuable —something that can't always be described exactly, or measured, or fully explained. But *something*.

When one of these luminous encounters take place, most people feel an impulse to preserve it, somehow. Some try to keep a tangible reminder: a flower, a photograph, a handkerchief, perhaps.

A writer tries to preserve it in words.

The Joy of the Here and Now

That morning, I remember, I woke to the sense of despondency and depression that had been troubling me for several days. There were no great crises in my life, just minor worries. The mail seemed to consist of nothing but bills. I had done some work that wasn't much good. I had agreed to attempt a job that I didn't like: I was afraid of it, really. In my bleak and self-pitying mood it seemed to me that I was trapped. If I looked back, there was the shadow of disappointment. If I looked ahead, there was the specter of failure. And where else was there to look?

For an hour or so I tried to work, but it was no good. Outside my window, the sea rolled green and gold. When the tide turned, the surf would begin to hammer on the outer bars, a mile or so offshore. There were no solutions to problems out there, but there was temporary escape. So abruptly, saying nothing to anyone, I left the house. And on the path leading down to the boat I met my friend the rabbi, walking his dogs.

Or rather, my acquaintance the rabbi. We didn't know each other well. In his seventies, recently retired, he had a wonderful face, clean-shaven and strong. Pacing along with his terriers on a tandem leash, he might have been an English country squire out for a stroll.

He glanced at the two long surf rods—I always carry a spare—and then at the skiff riding just offshore. "Fishing? Alone?"

I nodded, and spoke jokingly: "Want to come?"

He looked at me thoughtfully. "Do you want company?"

I stared at him, taken back. I was not at all sure that I wanted to share my flight with anyone. And I was quite sure that the rabbi knew as much about surf-fishing as I knew about the Talmud. Still, I *had* asked him. "It's chancy fishing," I said. "Wet and rough. Good fish or none. But if you'd really like to try it . . . ."

"That's very kind of you," he said with the odd courtliness that he had. "May I have ten minutes to change?"

"Take your time," I told him resignedly. "I have to catch some bait anyway."

When he was gone, I took the cast net from the boat and caught three mullet. Then I sat on the gunwale trying not to regret my invitation. I didn't see, really, how the rabbi could be happy on a wave-haunted sandbar a mile from shore. All sorts of things could go wrong. A prowling shark might scare him. A sea nettle might brush him with fingers of fire.

I waited. Around me everything was as familiar as my skin: the jade water, the greener marshes, the fierce Georgia sun, the gentle sky. The little boat was just a curved piece of Fiberglas, but she knew how to play tag with the sea. The rods were shabby and sea-stained, but the reels were oiled and bright. The engine was shedding its paint, but I knew its moods down to the last sullen hiccough. These were my toys, and ordinarily when things went wrong I could merge myself with them and be comforted. But today my awareness was dulled; my mind seemed far away; I took them for granted.

The rabbi came back, eager as a boy. The engine whined; the wake flared out behind. At the mouth of the inlet we took the first big roller at an angle, jumped the trough, and landed on the second with a spine-shivering crash. The explosion of spray was higher than our heads. I watched the rabbi, ready to throttle back, but his eyes were as bright as the sun dazzle around us. The roar of the engine was in my ears, but I could read his lips. "Marvelous!" he was saying. "Marvelous!"

The bar I had in mind was a ribbon of sand perhaps fifty yards wide. At high tide it disappeared altogether, and already the sea gnawed at its eastern edge like a wolf with a bone. Here in the white water, sometimes, the big bass swam. Sometimes not.

The anchor sank its iron teeth into the sand. Behind us, now, the houses on the horizon seemed dwarfed, remote, unreal. Ahead, the sea stretched away, unfettered, toward the bulge of Africa. Beyond the breakers, pelicans were fishing, grotesque and ungainly until their final plunge, then sharp and streamlined as arrowheads.

When we left the boat, the rabbi looked down in wonderment at the sculptured sand patterns under his feet. I told him that the waves made them when the bar was covered. "Marvelous!" He shook his head slowly. "The footprints of the sea." Halfway across the bar he found a shell and held it up with delight. "Look! It still has the sunrise in it!"

I had passed such shells a thousand times. Now, suddenly, looking at the flushed opalescence, I felt a kind of warmth, an easing of tension, a lessening of loneliness.

We came to the leaping surf. As I baited the hooks, I gave a short lecture on the mysteries of bait-casting, the art of letting the rod do the work, the importance of maintaining thumb-pressure on the reel to avoid the horrors of a backlash. The rabbi listened patiently, a teacher taught. "I'll make the first cast for you," I said. "Then you're on your own. If a fish strikes, back up slowly, wear him down, and slide him out on the beach. The drag is set so that he can't break the line. But keep the pressure on him."

The water swirled warm around our knees. Lead and hooks arched out in a long, lazy parabola and vanished. I handed over the rod, moved away, made my own cast. Silence, then, except for wind-hum and wave-slap, foam-hiss and bird-cry. I found myself thinking about the rabbi, groping for the essence of the man. There was something about him, something so simple yet so profound that I couldn't quite grasp it. Out of the corner of my eye I could see him, braced against the buffeting of the waves, face turned skyward to watch a gull riding the silver stream of the wind. He had let his rod tip drop until it was almost in the water. All wrong, but there was no use shouting at him. There is something about the surf that smothers voices.

Time passed. The rabbi managed a timid cast or two. The tide moved in, soon we would have to go. I glanced up and saw the rabbi making his way toward me, shaking his head. He held out his rod sorrowfully. I looked at the tangled mass of monofilament on his reel. A stupendous backlash. Unbelievable. "Can you fix it?"

I handed him my rod and took his. It was hopeless. Nothing but a sharp knife could fix it, and that sort of surgery takes time. I opened my mouth to tell him so. And in that instant the world changed. The rod in the rabbi's hands curved into a quivering bow. The reel shrieked. On his face, indescribably blended, were shock, consternation, incredulity, amazement. I knew how he felt. When a big bass strikes it's not as if a fish has taken your line. It's like having the ocean seize it.

The rabbi was holding on grimly, arms rigid, eyes wide. The fish ended its first desperate run; sixty yards away I saw it break water with an angry swirl and the flash of a great bronze tail. The rabbi was backing up now, toward the beach. He gained five yards of line, lost ten, then suddenly the fish turned and ran straight at him.

When the sea is holding your knees in a tight embrace, and you're leaning back against twenty pounds of pull, and that pressure is suddenly removed, the result is predictable. The rabbi fell over backwards. The sea rolled over him. No rod. No rabbi. Nothing.

But before I could move to help him he rose, dripping, from the foam. His cap had vanished; water poured from the pockets of his jacket. He groped in the depths for the rod. I knew that if the fish had taken up the slack, it would be gone. But he found it, gripped it, raised it aloft. The reel, violated by sand and salt water, moaned a metallic protest. The fish was still on.

He was still on, and now he made a great sweep to the south. The line hissed through the water like a scythe. The rabbi, turning to face his adversary, kept resolutely backing up. But now he was moving *away* from the beach. I had to flounder out and take him by the shoulders and turn him back.

Then there was nothing to do but wait and watch and hope that hook and leader would hold, that man would outlast fish. Twice more I saw forty inches of frenzied copper swirl beneath the surface, and each time I yelled and clapped my hands like a child, because the haze was gone from my mind and heart and I saw it as the rabbi was seeing it for the first time, all new and wonderful and splendid.

The great bass came in finally on the shoulders of a wave, head down, back arched, still full of fight. In his excitement, the rabbi dropped his rod tip until it was pointing straight at the fish. I gave a strangled cry of warning. Too late. The massive tail slammed against the sand as the bass reversed himself. There was no spring in the rod to cushion the shock. With a twang like a harp-string breaking, the leader snapped. Spray flashed like diamonds. He was gone.

I stood there, suspended in silence. The rabbi came up beside me. He was soaked, bedraggled, trembling, but there was no defeat in his eyes, no disappointment. "Marvelous!" he said hoarsely. "Marvelous!"

He rested one hand on my shoulder, and I felt how tired he was. "Come on, Rabbi," I said gently. "Let's go home."

Like a dream it all faded behind us, sun and salt, sand and sky. We came to the anchorage. On the shore my new friend turned and made a little formal bow. "Thank you," he said. "Thank you for one of the great mornings of my life."

"Thank *you*," I murmured.

I watched him go up the path through the dunes, and some of his phrases came echoing back to me—the footprints of the sea—the shell with sunrise in it. There was a kind of secret joy in them, and now I felt I knew what the secret was. This man didn't concern himself with looking forward or back. He didn't regret the past or flinch from the future. He lived in the present, the actual graspable moment of existence, the only point where true contact with reality is possible. And I thought of that other Rabbi who said,

Take therefore no thought for the morrow . . . .

I picked up the backlashed reel. With my knife I cut away the snarls and tangles, threw them over the side, watched them drift away. There was still plenty of line left. I put the boat in order. Then I went back, back to the demanding hours, back to the love and work and friends and family waiting for me in the marvelous here and now.

Runyon's Last Round

Whenever I walk by a certain hotel on Fifty-seventh Street in Manhattan, the past reaches out and taps me on the shoulder. I went into that hotel only once, and spent less than an hour there, but . . . .

It was in the winter of 1946. I had walked out of the air force into a magazine job of some consequence, and one of the items I found on my desk was a manuscript by Damon Runyon. The script had been bought and paid for, but I didn't think much of it. I had always admired Runyon's work; in fact, I considered him one of the truly great American short-story writers. But this effort seemed tired and careless and weak. And so, although I'd never met Runyon, I decided to ask him to rewrite it.

Knowing that his hotel was only a few blocks from our office, I asked my secretary to find out if it would be convenient for me to stop by and see him after work. Back came word that this would be satisfactory, so at about six o'clock I took the script and walked through the cold twilight to the hotel. If I had any qualms about telling one of the giants of contemporary fiction that his story wasn't much good, I don't remember them now. I had the raw, unabashed confidence of youth. Also, new brooms have a compulsion to sweep fanatically clean.

I got my first shock when Runyon opened the door of his suite. I recognized him instantly, from photographs I had seen. But nobody had warned me about his throat cancer. Nobody had informed me that he breathed through a tube masked by a bit of gauze at the base of his throat. Nobody, certainly, had told me that he was unable to speak a word, not even in a whisper.

He motioned for me to come in, and I did. The suite was small and untidy and rather dark, and there was something unhappy about it—something lonely. I found out later that Runyon had a friend who lived with him, a sort of male secretary who took messages and handled phone calls. But he was out. The two of us were alone.

Near the window was a table with a portable typewriter on it, and scraps of typescript lying around. There were two chairs, and Runyon indicated one of these. I sat down, feeling tension begin to build up inside me. Runyon twirled a sheet of paper into the machine and tapped out six words: WHAT CAN I DO FOR YOU?

For a moment I thought of backing down completely. I had not committed myself. It would have been very easy to say that I had always wanted to meet him (which was true) add something complimentary about his past work, and make a graceful exit. But I didn't. I put the manuscript on the table between us, and my nervousness made me three times as blunt as I had intended to be. I said, "Mr. Runyon, I don't think this is very good."

I saw the already-grim mouth tighten, the eyes behind the horn-rimmed glasses go cold, a red flush creep up the broad forehead. Later I was to learn that writing the story hadn't been Runyon's idea. He had been bribed and badgered until finally, more to rid himself of the incessant editorial pressure than anything else, he had wearily undertaken it. But I didn't know this then. All I knew was that he was angry.

He was angry, but he couldn't express the anger. All the searing words that must have flashed through his mind were dammed up there because of the cancer that had him by the throat. He was silent because he had to be silent, but all the same I felt his anger like a blow.

He clenched his fist once. Then, very calmly, he hit the spacing lever of the typewriter and wrote another line: WHAT'S WRONG WITH IT?

I knew, by this time, that I was making a terrible mistake. That he was sick, and lonely, and unhappy. That he had done the job as well as he could do it with the vitality that was left to him. I knew nothing about his personal life or the sadness that dwelt there, but I could sense it. I could sense, too, a kind of basic fear in him that could have been only one thing: the fear of extinction, the fear of approaching death. And this was reinforcing his anger, because fear and anger are never very far apart. And, in a way, I was a messenger, reminding him of all the grim, inevitable things he wanted to forget.

But I had gone too far, now, to turn back. So I told him what was wrong with the manuscript. I told him, and technically what I said was entirely true, but the fact that it was true just made it worse for both of us. Here was a man whose best work would be read and remembered for generations. Who was I to tell him what was good or bad? Why should he accept criticism from a stranger less than half his age, of no reputation or distinction? Why?

He did not accept it. He shook his head, mute and furious. With jaw muscles clenched, he hammered out explosive negatives that sounded like bursts of machine-gun fire: NO! DISAGREE! THAT'S ABSURD! NO!

The thing was becoming a nightmare for both of us. I got the impression that he did not dare admit that anything was wrong with the story, that such an admission would be devastating to him—somehow final. We were near the window, and the cold winter night was outside, but my shirt became soaked with perspiration. I felt as if the truth had been put into my hands as a weapon, and that I was using it against a man who could not defend himself. It was like fighting a man with both hands tied behind him. After a while you wish that your hands were tied too.

I stuck doggedly to my point that the script needed revision. REWRITE IT YOURSELF the typewriter snarled. At least I had sense enough to know that nobody could rewrite Runyon, and I said so. He slammed his hand down on the manuscript; the typewriter sputtered again: IT *is* RUNYON; WHAT MORE DO YOU WANT?

I did something then that was cruel, I suppose, but I was almost as upset as he was, and when your nerves are stretched that far you don't think very clearly. I couldn't bring myself to say it in words, but I pulled the typewriter away from him and wrote five words that summed it all up: I WANT THE OLD RUNYON!

He flicked a glance at the sentence, then he looked at me. I can still remember how the silence sang in the room. And suddenly he must have seen how young and frightened and miserable I really was, because a change came over his face. A remarkable change. The anger died out of it, the steel-trap mouth relaxed, a wry, resigned humor came into his eyes. He turned the typewriter sideways, so that I could read, and this time he typed slowly: THE OLD RUNYON DOESN'T LIVE HERE ANYMORE . . . . He glanced up again, then went on: . . . BUT IF YOU SAY SO, I'LL TRY.

And he did. He didn't make the story much better, but that isn't the point. The point is that he tried. He was sick and lonely and tired and dying—but he tried.

I still have that piece of paper somewhere, with the words we both typed on it. And maybe Damon was right in thinking that the magic was gone from his typewriter. But he was wrong about one thing.

The old Runyon did live there. He lived there until he died.

The Beginning

The September morning was calm and bright. The town looked fresh and shining and very American. We drove slowly through the gilded streets, not saying anything.

Sherry sat beside me, scrubbed and solemn. We had decided, her mother and I, not to make anything momentous of this first day at school. I was to drop her there and drive on. She knew which classroom was hers. We had all inspected it the week before.

Symbolically, perhaps, the school was on a hill. A flight of steps rose from the street, bisecting the green lawn, arrowing straight to the wide door centered in the red-brick Colonial building. A public school. A good one, so they said.

Already a trickle of small humanity was flowing up the steps. It was easy to spot the first-graders. Most of them were anchored to their mothers' hands. I glanced at Sherry. She was staring at her lap.

"We're a little early," I said. "Want to sit here for a couple of minutes?"

She nodded. I leaned forward and cut the ignition. I had not expected to feel anything, but now I felt a queer breathlessness, as if I were waiting for something important to happen.

Sherry smoothed her dress carefully over her knees. The part in her hair looked very straight and white. *What is she thinking*, I asked myself suddenly. *What goes on inside that bright, new, untouched mind? Does she know what it means, this first step on the endless ladder of education? Does she have any idea? Of course she doesn't,* I told myself impatiently. *If she did, she'd probably jump out of the car and run away. How many years of classrooms? Twelve, at least. Sixteen, if she goes to college. More, if she chooses a profession.*

I gripped the wheel tighter, thinking of all the unknown individuals who would try to teach this child and in trying would leave some mark, however tiny, on her mind or her heart. Frightening, somehow. Terrifying, almost.

Sherry lifted one foot and examined the scissor scratches on the sole of her new shoe. *They will explain the physical world to you,* I thought. *They may show you how to blueprint the atom. They may give you a map of the spiral nebulae. But who will help you know yourself? Who will teach you to chart your own emotions? Who will offer you a guide to the frail complexities of the human spirit? Nobody, nobody . . . .*

Try to learn their facts, I said to Sherry in my mind, *but don't worry too much if you can't. You'll forget most of them anyway, sooner or later. I memorized the quadratic formula once, and read all the plays of Molière in the original. What earthly good it did me I still don't know. The things that matter you won't learn from any blackboard. That I can promise you.*

A knot of small male animals went by, full of raucous high spirits. *There go your real teachers, Sherry,* I said to her silently. *Take a good look at them, your contemporaries. They will teach you many things that are not in any schoolbooks. Unpleasant things sometimes. How to lie, how to cheat, God knows what else . . . .*

Maybe you have to learn those things before you can also learn that ultimately they're not worth doing. I don't know. I'm your father, and you think I know everything, but you're wrong. All I really know is that I don't know much—and when you make that discovery about yourself someday, why then the first part of your education will be complete.

But they won't teach you that in school, either. If they did, much of the importance of what they're doing with all their chalk and books and rulers would melt away, and that would never do.

The happy savages went whooping up the steps. Sherry watched them, and I watched Sherry. *Five minutes from now,* I thought, *you won't be just you anymore. You'll also be one of them. It may be the biggest step you'll ever take. I hope it's in the right direction.*

I looked at the school high on the hill and the open door with the little figures going into it, and a clammy doubt seized me, a doubt as to the ultimate wisdom of pouring these young lives into such a mold, however good, however well intentioned. Conformity, regimentation, the desire not to be different but to be as much like everyone else as possible—was this *really* the way to develop independence, originality, leadership?

No such school system existed when our country was born. Yet consider the genius that blazed forth in those days. Washington, Jefferson, Franklin, Hamilton, John Marshall, Patrick Henry—all these and many more from a tiny nation of barely 3 million souls. Now we number 200 million, and schools and colleges cover the land. But where are the leaders, where are the men?

I glanced again at the child beside me. *Maybe it doesn't matter,* I thought, *maybe the pattern is already set. Maybe the seeds of personality are already planted and nothing can alter the way they will grow. Maybe—I don't know. One more thing I don't know.*

Anyway, I said to myself, *the time has come. Open that tight parental hand and let her go. It's her life, remember, not yours.*

I reached across her and opened the door. She got out slowly and stood with her back to me, looking up at the building on the hill. Now I was supposed to drive nonchalantly away.

"So long, Sherry," I said.

She turned her head, and suddenly that wonderful flood of love and humor came up behind her eyes.

"Don't be scared, Daddy," she said. "I'll be back." And she went climbing up into the blue infinity of the morning.

Message From the Sea

Some people in this world have a marvelous gift. It's hard to say exactly what this quality is: a serenity, an inner strength, a generosity of spirit. Whatever it is, when you're in trouble, or have some aching problem, you turn to these people instinctively. Something in them draws you like a magnet. I have a friend like that. So, the other night, when something was weighing on my mind, I telephoned him.

"Come on over," he said. "Alma's gone to bed, and I was about to heat up some coffee."

So I went over, and at the end of an hour—just as I knew I would—I felt a lot better. The problem was still there, but somehow it didn't seem so frightening. Not with Ken sitting in his old swivel chair, feet up on the desk, hands locked behind his head, not saying much, just listening . . . and *caring*.

Suddenly the gratitude and affection I felt seemed to need expression. "Ken," I said, "when it comes to smoothing out wrinkles in troubled minds, you're wonderful. How do you do it?"

He has a slow smile that seems to start in his eyes. "Well," he said, "I'm a good deal older than you."

I shook my head. "Age has nothing to do with it. There's a calmness in you that goes very deep. Where did you get it?"

He looked at me pensively for a few seconds, as if trying to make up his mind whether to tell me something. Finally, with the toe of his shoe, he pulled open one of the desk drawers. From it he took a small cardboard box. He put it on the blotter. "If I do have any of this quality you're talking about," he said, "it probably comes from this."

I waited. On the mantel a clock ticked.

Ken picked up one of his blackened pipes and began to load it. "You've known me for . . . how long? ten years? twelve? This box is a lot older than that. I've had it more than thirty years. Alma is the only other person who knows what's in it, and maybe she has forgotten. But I take it out and look at it now and then."

The match flared; the smoke curled, blue and reflective, in the lamplight. "Back in the '20s," Ken said in a faraway voice, "I was a successful young man in New York. Successful as hell. I made money fast and spent it faster. I was the golden boy, able to outthink or outdrink anybody. I married Alma because she was pretty and decorative, but I don't think I loved her. I don't think there was any love in me, really. The closest thing to it was the very high regard that I had—for myself."

I stared at him in amazement. I found it almost impossible to believe this brutal self-portrait.

"Well," said Ken, "as you've probably anticipated, the day of reckoning came. And it was quite a day. It's hard for people who didn't go through the Wall Street crash to know what it was like. One week I was a millionaire—on paper, anyway. The next I was a pauper. My reaction was predictable: I got drunk and stayed drunk for three days."

He gave a short bark of a laugh and stood up, running a hand through his wiry hair. "The place I chose for this little orgy of self-pity was a beach cottage that we owned—or, rather, had owned before the bottom fell out of our gilded cage. Alma wanted to come with me, but I wouldn't let her. I just wanted to get away from everything and drink myself blind, and I did.

"But the time comes when you begin to sober up. For an

alcoholic—and I was close to being one—this can be a ghastly experience. You're overwhelmed with self-disgust; you're choked with despair. I looked at my face in the mirror, the bloodshot eyes, the three-day beard, and knew I was looking at a total failure. As a man, as a husband, as a human being, I had made a complete mess of my life. The thought—no, it wasn't a thought, it was a conviction—the conviction came to me that the best thing I could do for Alma and for everyone else would be to remove myself from the scene, permanently.

"I knew, moreover, just how to do it. A half-gale was blowing outside. The sea was wild. I would swim out as far as I could, past the point of no return. That would take care of everything."

Ken's pipe had gone out; he put it on the desk. The old chair creaked as he sat down. "When you're driven to a decision like that, your one thought is to get it over with. So I wasted no time. I stumbled down the porch steps and onto the beach. It was just after dawn, I remember; the sky was red and angry; the waves were furious. I walked straight to the edge of the water. As I reached it, something glinted on the sand." He opened the box. "This."

In the box was a shell. Not a particularly unusual shell; I had seen others like it. A narrow oval of fluted calcium, pale, graceful, delicate.

"I stood there staring at it," Ken went on. "Finally I picked it up, wet and glistening. It was so fragile that the least pressure of my fingers would have crushed it. Yet here it was, undamaged, perfect.

"How was this possible? The question seemed to seize upon my mind, while all around me the wind shrieked and the ocean roared. Tons of seething water had flung this shell on the hard-packed sand. It should have been smashed to splinters, utterly destroyed. But it wasn't.

"What had kept the shell intact, unbroken? I kept asking

myself this question with a kind of frantic urgency—and suddenly I knew. It had yielded itself to the awful forces crashing around it. It had accepted the storm just as it had accepted the stillness of the depths where it had had its beginnings. And it had survived.

"I don't know how long I stood there, but finally, when I turned away from the sea, I took the shell with me. I've had it ever since."

I took the box from my friend and lifted out the shell. It lay in my hand, untouched by the years, exquisitely wrought, featherlight. "Do you know its name?" I asked.

Ken smiled that slow smile of his. "Yes," he said. "They call it an angel's wing."

Answer at Nightfall

Sometimes I think, a bit wryly, that a parent can't really teach children anything of importance; all you can do is expose them to living. That way the lessons come so quietly and unobtrusively that often you aren't aware of them, until you begin to think back.

Yesterday, for example . . . .

We were returning, the four of us, from an hour of late-afternoon fishing. Our little skiff took the rollers easily, gold-flecked in the burnished light. To our left, the low dunes of the Georgia coast. To our right, nothing but birds and sea and sky, and now and then the quicksilver flash of a leaping mackerel. Ordinarily we would have been five in the boat. But Dana, our fourteen-year-old lover-of-all-living-things, had elected to stay at home with a baby raccoon she had somehow acquired. "I have to fix his formula," she had said happily. "Besides, if I leave him, he squeaks."

I decided to land my crew—one wife, two children—and let them walk home while I took the boat to its anchorage up an inlet. As we eased in to the beach, I noticed a pelican on the sand near the water's edge, huddled and motionless. He watched us as we approached, but made no attempt to fly.

"That bird doesn't seem very happy," I said, and thought no more about it until I arrived home after mooring the boat. At the foot of our steps, head drooping, great wings half-spread, was the pelican. Around him, silhouettes of concern, were the members of my family—now including Dana, who crouched close, blond hair falling across her face, sunburned arms protectively around the bird's neck. She looked up, her gray eyes misty. "Oh, Daddy," she said, "what's wrong with him? He can't fly, and he can hardly walk, and he's shivering."

I resisted an impulse to say that, no matter what was wrong with him, a family with eight cats and a poodle and a baby raccoon hardly needed any more animal problems. My wife, as usual, read my mind. "We couldn't just walk away and leave him," she said quietly.

"We carried him all the way," our youngest said proudly. "I carried his head and part of his neck, and he didn't even try to bite!"

I looked at the great bill with a hook at the end, so light yet so strong, and thought—not for the first time—how strange and marvelous it was that a creature so grotesque could know one moment of flashing beauty: at the last split-second of his dive, a fishing pelican folds his clumsy wings and cleaves the water like a hurled javelin, all grace and power and precision. But I had a feeling that this bird would know such moments no more.

I ran my hand along the silky throat feathers. I could feel no obstruction. The bird flinched a little, took a few floundering steps and then grew still, yellow eyes watching us remotely. "Maybe," I said, "we should call the vet."

"We did," my wife told me. "He said that about all we could do for tonight was give him some water and watch him."

"He doesn't want water," Dana said sadly. "He doesn't want bread, either. I offered him some."

"We can cut up some fish," I said. "But I doubt if he'll eat any."

We offered the fish; it was ignored. We poured a little water into the corners of the unresisting bill. He did not seem afraid of us, but now and then convulsive tremors ran through him. "Oh, he's cold," wailed Dana, and pinned a beach towel tenderly around him.

The sun went down in a smear of crimson. The others finally went inside to supper, leaving Dana and me alone with the bird. Out over the ocean, seeking their night resting places, long lines of pelicans were arching across the sky, and I wondered if the earthbound one was aware of them. "Let's take him back down to the water," I said at last to Dana. "When he sees all his friends going home, maybe he'll try to go with them."

With Dana carrying the huge, passive bird, we walked down to the seawall, through the dunes, across the deserted beach. The tide was ebbing; the waves were steel-colored in the fading light. Almost above us now, from south to north, the silent wings swept past. Dana waded out ankle-deep. I watched as she unpinned the towel and put her burden down. And it was very strange: as if on signal, at the instant the broad webbed feet touched the water, something was released, something ended. Without a sound, the great, ungainly head fell forward into the waves. "Bring him back, baby," I said gently. "He's dead."

She brought him back and laid him on the sand, somehow smaller, very quiet, very still. She knelt beside him, tears streaming down her face. "Oh," she said to him in an anguished voice, "why did you do that? Why did you have to die?"

The wind blew, and the waves moved in, and the question hung in the air as it has since the beginning of time.

"Don't be sad," I said at last. "He's not sick or unhappy anymore."

She drew a long breath and wiped her eyes with the back of her hand. She looked up at the great procession overhead. "Do you think any of his children are up there?"

"Probably. Children and grandchildren and great-grandchildren."

She nodded slowly, eyes shadowed with the mystery and miracle of death and life. She reached out once and smoothed the damp feathers gently. Then she stood up and shook back her hair. "Can we bury him now?" We buried him at the foot of the dunes where the melancholy sea oats could watch over him. I shaped a mound and put some broken pieces of concrete on top. The tides would never reach this far.

At the seawall we looked back to where the concrete glimmered. Then Dana spoke softly. To me or to herself? "He *was* back where he wanted to be, wasn't he? And he *is* still part of it, isn't he?"

The stars were beginning to show through; the sea was dark; the birds were gone in the gathering night. My daughter took my hand with grown-up firmness. "Let's go in now," she said, "and see about feeding that hungry raccoon."

6

The Gift of Awareness

Great men have always stressed the value of wonder. "Two things," wrote Immanuel Kant, "fill the mind with ever-increasing wonder and awe . . . the starry heavens above me and the moral law within me." Albert Einstein said, "The most beautiful thing we can experience is the mysterious." Thomas Carlyle pointed out that wonder is the basis of worship.

How do we keep in the forefront of our minds the simple fact that we live in an indescribably wonderful world? It's not easy. Routine dulls the eye and ear. Repetition and familiarity fog the capacity for astonishment. Even so, moments come to all of us when everything suddenly seems fresh and new and marvelous.

This gift of awareness makes possible some of our happiest hours. We need to be receptive to it and grateful for it because, as the poet John Masefield once wrote, "The days that make us happy make us wise."

The Night the Stars Fell

One summer night in a seaside cottage, a small boy felt himself lifted from bed. Dazed with sleep, he heard his mother murmur about the lateness of the hour, heard his father laugh. Then he was borne in his father's arms, with the swiftness of a dream, down the porch steps, out onto the beach.

Overhead the sky blazed with stars. "Watch!" his father said. And incredibly, as he spoke, one of the stars moved. In a streak of golden fire, it flashed across the astonished heavens. And before the wonder of this could fade, another star leaped from its place, and then another, plunging toward the restless sea. "What is it?" the child whispered. "Shooting stars," his father said. "They come every year on certain nights in August. I thought you'd like to see the show."

That was all: just an unexpected glimpse of something haunting and mysterious and beautiful. But, back in bed, the child stared for a long time into the dark, rapt with the knowledge that all around the quiet house the night was full of the silent music of the falling stars.

Decades have passed, but I remember that night still, because I was the fortunate seven-year-old whose father believed that a new experience was more important for a small boy than an unbroken night's sleep. No doubt in my childhood I had the usual quota of playthings, but these are forgotten now. What I remember is the night the stars fell, the day we rode in a caboose, the time we tried to skin the alligator, the telegraph we made that really worked. I remember the trophy table in the hall where we children were encouraged to exhibit things we had found—snake skins, seashells, flowers, arrowheads—anything unusual or beautiful.

I remember the books left by my bed that pushed back my horizons and sometimes actually changed my life. Once my father gave me *Zuleika Dobson,* Max Beerbohm's classic story of undergraduate life at Oxford. I liked it, and told him so. "Why don't you think about going there yourself?" he said casually. A few years later—with luck and a scholarship—I did.

My father had, to a marvelous degree, the gift of opening doors for his children, of leading them into areas of splendid newness. This subtle art of adding dimensions to a child's world doesn't necessarily require a great deal of time. It simply involves doing things more often with our children instead of for them or to them. One woman I know keeps what she calls a "Why not?" notebook, and in it she scribbles all sorts of offbeat and fascinating proposals: "Why not take kids police headquarters—get them finger-printed?" "Why not visit farm—attempt milk cow?" "Why not arrange ride tugboat?" "Why not follow river dredge and hunt for fossilized shark's teeth?" And so they do.

One day I asked her where she got her ideas. "Oh," she said, "I don't know. But when I was a child, I had this wonderful old ne'er-do-well uncle who . . . ." who used to open doors for her, just as she is opening them now for her own children.

Aside from our father, we had a remarkable aunt who was a genius at suggesting spur-of-the-moment plots to blow away the dust of daily drudgeries. "Can you stand on your head?" she would ask us children. "I can!" And, tucking her skirt between her knees, she would do so. "What shall we do this afternoon?" she would cry, and answer her own question instantly: "Let's have our fortunes told!" Always a new dimension, always a magic door opening, an experience to be shared. That's the key word: we *shared*.

Along with these excursions came little unpremeditated revelations of character that could not fail to leave a mark on our impressionable minds. Once, I remember, our adventurous aunt arranged for us to ride a pony that was a bit skittish. After being thrown three times, my brother protested tearfully that riding this particular animal was too difficult. "If it were too easy," our aunt said serenely, "it wouldn't be any fun." Just a casual phrase, but it sticks in my memory.

The easiest door to open for a child, usually, is one that leads to something you love yourself. All good teachers know this. And all good teachers know the ultimate reward: the marvelous moment when the spark you are breathing on bursts into a flame that henceforth will burn brightly on its own. At a United States Golf Association tournament a few years ago, a pigtailed ten-year-old played creditably in the junior girls' championship. "How long have you been interested in golf?" someone asked her. "I got it for my ninth birthday," she said. "You mean your father gave you a set of clubs?" "No," she said patiently, "he gave me *golf*."

The possessor of a wonderful realm had wanted his child to share the magic kingdom. No doubt it took some time and effort, some patience, some mystical transference of enthusiasm. But what a reward for both of them! And it might just as well have been music or astronomy or chemistry or collecting butterflies—any world at all.

Children are naturally inquisitive and love to try new things. But they cannot find these things by themselves; someone must offer them the choices. Years ago, when the

Quiz Kids were astonishing American radio audiences with their brilliance, a writer set out to discover what common denominators there were in the backgrounds of these extraordinary children. He found that some were from poor families, some from rich; some had been to superior schools, some had not.

But, in every case investigated, there was one parent, sometimes two, who shared enthusiasms with the child, who watched for areas of interest, who gave encouragement and praise for achievement, who made a game of searching out the answers to questions, who went out of his way to supply the tools of learning. No doubt the capacity for outstanding performance was already there, but it took the love and interest and companionship of a parent to bring it out.

Recently a neighbor of ours took his two small children to the mountains for a vacation. The very first morning the children woke him at daybreak, clamoring to go exploring. Stifling an impulse to send them back to bed, he struggled into his clothes and took them for a walk. At the edge of a pond they stopped to rest and while they were sitting there quietly a doe and her fawn came down to drink.

"I watched my youngsters' faces," he said, "and suddenly it was as if I were seeing and feeling everything for the first time: the hush of the woods, the mist over the water, the grace and gentleness of those lovely creatures, the kinship of all living things. It only lasted a few seconds, but the thought came to me that happiness isn't something you have to strive and struggle for. It's simply an awareness of the beauty and harmony of existence. And I said to myself: Remember this moment, put it away carefully in your mind—because you may need to draw strength and comfort from it some day." Giving his children a new experience, that man also opened a door for himself.

I have a friend, a psychiatrist, who says that basically

there are two types of human beings: those who think of life as a privilege and those who think of it as a problem. The first type is enthusiastic, energetic, resistant to shock, responsive to challenge. The other type is suspicious, hesitant, withholding, self-centered. To the first group, life is hopeful, exciting. To the second, it's a potential ambush. And he adds, "Tell me what sort of childhood you had and I can tell you which type you are likely to be."

The real purpose, then, of trying to open doors for children is not to divert them or amuse ourselves; it is to build eager, outgoing attitudes toward the demanding and complicated business of living. This, surely, is the most valuable legacy we can pass on to the next generation: not money, not houses or heirlooms, but a capacity for wonder and gratitude, a sense of aliveness and joy. Why don't we work harder at it? Probably because, as Thoreau said, our lives are frittered away by detail. Because there are times when we don't have the awareness or the selflessness or the energy.

And yet, for those of us who care what becomes of our children, the challenge is always there. None of us meets it fully, but the opportunities come again and again. Many years have passed since that night in my life when the stars fell, but the earth still turns, the sun still sets, night still sweeps over the changeless sea. And next year, when August comes with its shooting stars, *my* son will be seven.

The Day We Almost Didn't Go

Almost—almost—we didn't go. The afternoon was right for it: clear, not cold, a veil of sand blowing off the lion-colored dunes and whispering into the restless sea along our strip of Georgia coast. And all the three youngest children wanted was for me to take them across the river and through the winding tidal creeks to the deserted beaches farther south where they could look for shells or follow coon tracks or gather sea oats or watch for wild goats.

Simple, really: a fifteen-minute run in our little outboard skiff. But the tide was out, and the boat would be stranded, and getting it into the water would be a struggle. Besides, there was a televised football game that promised a degree of entertainment with much less effort. So I had said, "We'll see," in the vague tone that parents use. And the children knew from long experience that this means *no*.

But then I saw their forlorn faces, as they huddled in a disconsolate triangle.

"All right," I said, feeling noble and exasperated and self-sacrificing. "All *right*. We'll go. But just for a little while."

Faces brightened. "Can we take Tony?" Tony is a Shetland sheep dog, unacquainted with sheep, who loves boats.

"I guess so," I said. And automatically, "Wear something warm."

Down at the river, we dragged the boat to the water,

getting muddy feet. The engine coughed morosely for a while, then picked up with a splendid roar and drove us through the chop so fast that spray soaked everyone, including the sheltie, who stood in the bow, ears pinned back by the wind, tongue waving with delight.

For three minutes the skiff pranced and bucked in the river. Then suddenly we were in the sheltered network of creeks, skimming around silver corners, flying down amber aisles of marsh grass where blackbirds flared in silent explosions, past dead trees pointing like witches, finally into a broad estuary where the engine bellowed happily at full throttle.

Ahead of us now I could see leaping tongues of surf above the strip of barrier beach, and far away on some high dunes to the southeast a handful of goats moving slowly with a kind of lordly assurance as if the realities we knew could never touch them. I pointed, wordless against the clamor of the engine. Everyone looked and nodded gravely. The world had not changed. The goats were still there.

The skiff eased into a quiet cove. I cut the engine, and at once the surf thundered in our ears. The dog sprang ashore and sank to his astonished chin in damp and porous sand. The children floundered after him, carrying the anchor as they had been taught. A fearsome crew, really. Kinzie, thirteen, was wearing blue jeans scissored off raggedly at the knee; on her head a once-white sailor hat with down-turned brim was pulled so low that she looked like a candle being snuffed. Dana, eleven, wore an old cashmere sweater of mine, full of holes, with sleeves so long that she seemed to have no hands at all, but her eyes were the color of seawater on a cloudy day, and her hair was a mermaid-meteor in the wind. Mac, eight, wore a sweatshirt with an improbable-looking bulldog stenciled on it. As always, he needed a haircut.

They raced away through the sea oats, so many things to find or do (and take for granted): fiddler crabs to catch and carry home to be harnessed with thread and coaxed to pull paper chariots; marsh swallows' nests, sometimes with eggs; skeletons of rowboats resting their weary bones against the dunes; floats from seine nets, starfish and sand dollars, conchs' eggs and horseshoe crabs, all flung carelessly by the lavish hand of the sea. I watched them go with tolerance and amusement, I, too, a taker-for-granted, and with less excuse—none, really, except that most of the time that's what all parents tend to be where their children are concerned.

I was tilting the engine to keep the propeller out of the sand when I heard the sheltie barking, hysterical high-pitched yelps coming fast downwind. A moment later Mac came rushing back, eyes dark with excitement. "Daddy, come quick . . . a bird, a big one, maybe a goose . . . he can't fly . . . he's hurt or something . . . *hurry!*"

Through the soft sand, heavy-footed, into the dune grasses, up over the shallow rise, and there on the beach, shadows against the sun dazzle, the two girls and the sheltie surrounding a strange, penguinlike silhouette that lurched and flopped awkwardly, long neck and javelin bill lunging defiantly at the dog. I came close and saw the webbed feet set too far back for walking, the sleek head, and the angry eyes. It was a loon, feathers matted into a hopeless, tarry mass. Looking at it, I felt something wince inside me: The worst that can happen to any creature is to be made incapable of doing the thing it was created to do.

"What's wrong with him?" cried Dana, not far from tears.

"He got too close to civilization," I said slowly. And I told them how sometimes a ship discharges fuel oil that makes a heavy slick on the ocean, and how a diving loon might come up under this deadly film and have its plumage so saturated that it could not fly.

"Will he be all right?" Mac asked fearfully. "What will happen to him?"

I knew that after sundown a roving raccoon would answer these questions, and that nature's solution would be better than slow death by starvation, but I could not bring myself to say so.

"There's a towel in the boat," said Kinzie, the practical one. "Maybe we can wipe him off."

"He'll bite us!" cried Mac with delight and terror.

"Not very hard," I said. "Get the towel. We'll give it a try."

But even when I held the proud head so that the dagger bill could not strike, and pinioned the strong but useless wings, the towel made little impression. "We need something to dissolve the oil," I said finally. "Mineral spirits, maybe."

"There's some at home," both girls said at once.

"Let's take him home!" shouted their brother deliriously. "We'll clean him up and put him in the bathtub and feed him some dog food and make him a pet!"

"He's a wild bird," I said, some obscure parental resistance rising up in me. "He doesn't want to live in a bathtub and be a pet. Besides, I'm not sure we can get this stuff off."

"But we *found* him," Kinzie said a little desperately. "We can't just leave him here to die."

We found him, that was true—or perhaps he found us. Either way, out of all the millions of possible space-time curves, something had caused his and ours to intersect in this unlikely place. Chance? Of course. But still . . . .

"Who'll hold him?" I asked a bit grumpily. "I can't run a

boat with one hand and hang onto a wild loon with the other."

"I'll hold him," all three of them said instantly. And they did (or at least the older girl did, the others close on either side), the bird wrapped firmly with a corner of the towel over its head (which seemed to quiet it), and the sheltie crouched, disapproving and dejected, at my feet.

"We've got a loon!" Mac shrieked to his unsuspecting mother as we entered the house. "An oily one! We're going to wash him in the bathtub!" He hesitated, his masculine radar picking up dubious vibrations. "But then," he added more quietly, "we're going to let him go."

The next hour was chaotic. Preparations were immense: sponges, cotton pads, warm water, cool water, soaps, elixirs and combinations of elixirs. Theories were advanced and demolished. Advice was endless. The loon, unappreciative, bit everyone at least twice. And traces of oil clung grimly. But finally, when the last rinse disappeared from the stained tub, the dark feathers were parallel and distinguishable, and most of the weighted clumsiness was gone.

We took him, wrapped in a clean towel, through the living room, down the porch steps, across the dusky beach to the ocean's edge. When we put him in the water, he bobbed uncertainly for a moment. He turned his head and raked his back feathers swiftly with his bill, as if to align them properly. Then he started swimming strongly out to sea, toward the distant sandbar where shorebirds were settling for the night.

"Why doesn't he fly?" Dana asked worriedly.

"I think his feathers are too wet," I said. "When the sun dries them tomorrow, he may be all right."

The sheltie, spirits revived, went bounding off, and the girls followed him. The boy and I turned back toward the house, crouching in the dunes, its roof line sharp against the western sky. The sand squeaked as he scuffed his feet. "He would have died, wouldn't he, Daddy?"

"Yes, he would."

He shook his head slowly. "And we almost didn't go, remember?"

"Yes," I said. "Yes, I'll try to remember."

The Deadly Art of Nonliving

One raw, cold day last winter I found myself having lunch at the seaside cottage of some friends, an attractive young couple in their twenties. The only other guest was a retired college professor, a marvelous old gentleman, still straight as a lance after seven decades of living. We had planned a walk on the beach after lunch. But as gusts of wind shook the house and occasional pellets of sleet hissed against the windows, our hosts' enthusiasm dwindled visibly.

"Sorry," said the wife, "but nobody's going to get me out of the house in this weather." "That's right," her husband agreed comfortably. "Why risk pneumonia when you can sit by the fire and watch the world go by on televison?"

We left them, finally, preparing to do just that. But when we came to our cars, parked some distance away, I was astonished to see the professor open the trunk of his ancient sedan and take out an ax. "Lots of lovely driftwood out there," he said, gesturing toward the windswept beach. "Think I'll get a load for my fireplace."

I stared at him. "You're going out there to chop wood? On this sort of afternoon?"

He gave me a quizzical look. "Why not?" he said. "It's better than practicing the deadly art of nonliving, isn't it?" And with the ax slanted across one shoulder, he set off through the dunes.

I watched him go with the sudden odd feeling that something was wrong here, something curiously inverted in the proper order of things. Two youngsters were content to sit placidly by the fire; an old man was striding off jauntily into an icy wind; and I myself was left with a choice—an obscurely important choice—and precious little time to make it.

"Wait!" I heard myself calling to him. "Wait, I'm coming!"

A small episode, to be sure. We chopped some armfuls of wood. We loaded them into his car. We got a bit wet, but not cold. There was a kind of exhilaration about it all, the ax blade biting into the weathered timbers, the chips flying, the sea snarling in the background. And a kind of unspoken, unexpected intimacy, too. But what really stuck in my mind was that phrase about the deadly art of nonliving, because I think the old professor put his finger on one of the most insidious maladies of our time: the tendency in most of us to observe rather than act, avoid rather than participate, not-do rather than do; the tendency to give in to the sly, negative, cautionary voices that constantly counsel us to be careful, to be controlled, to be wary and prudent and hesitant and guarded in our approach to this complicated thing called living.

I always look with a certain amount of suspicion on people who claim that the world is getting worse, not better. But in this particular area, at least where Americans are concerned, I think the claim may well be true. We *are* more inert than our ancestors, and cleverer at inventing excuses for indolence. "Why risk pneumonia?" our host asked jovially. There was no real risk of pneumonia, and all of us knew it. But almost without thinking, he spoke three words that supplied him with a neat little justification for inertia.

The trouble is, people are much more standardized than they used to be. Perhaps because life is easier, they no longer hurl themselves at it the way their forebears did.

Eccentricity has virtually vanished from the American scene. Extravagance of any kind, emotional, physical or financial, is suspect. Far from burning any candles at both ends, more and more descendants of the pioneers seem to be reluctant even to light a match.

Part of the blame, without much doubt, can be laid squarely on the doorstep of overprotective parents. In hundreds of thousands of homes, I'm convinced, well-meaning fathers and mothers blunt their children's eagerness and sense of adventure with endless barrage of don'ts: "Don't climb that tree, you might fall out." "Don't go out in that canoe; you might drown." "No, you can't camp out this weekend, it might rain." The drive to live is a leaping flame in most children, but it can't survive an endless succession of wet blankets.

Another reason, probably, is the cumulative effect of the somber statistics constantly dinned into our ears by scientists, sociologists, and modern medicine men of all kinds. Our ancestors were mercifully free from these merchants of doom. Nobody warned our grandparents that they had better watch every drink because one out of fifteen social drinkers becomes an alcoholic. Nobody threatened them with creeping dissolution if they didn't stop smoking. Nobody urged them to ease up on weekend recreation because of the threat of heart failure. Maybe some of them did die off a bit sooner than people today but I wonder if they didn't get more fun out of life while they were at it.

Today, once you cross the threshold of the middle years, everywhere you look someone is separating himself from some activity or pleasure because someone else has convinced him that the divorce is good for him. And the disease of nonliving can be progressive. A contemporary of mine who gave up tennis several years ago because he feared it might be bad for his arteries has now taken to going to bed every night at nine o'clock. When you ask him why, he says he needs his rest; and to be fair about it he does look remarkably rested at all times. But you can't help wondering what he plans to do with all the energy he's conserving.

On my car radio the other day I heard a program that featured an interview with two centenarians. They were being asked the traditional questions about what had enabled them to reach the century mark, how they had celebrated their hundredth anniversary, and so on. One revealed that he had spent each of his last eighty birthdays in a tavern, and intended to maintain this merry tradition as long as he could. The other attributed his longevity to careful eating habits, no drinking, no smoking, never a cross word, and so on. He added that he had spent his hundredth birthday in bed, convalescing. "Convalescing from what?" growled the first old warrior. He had a point.

The point is that the march of science has handed us all such bonuses in health and energy and life-span that we should be living hugely, with enormous gusto and enjoyment, not tiptoeing through the years as if we were treading on eggs. For thousands of decades, man's chief concern was simply to survive, and he seldom succeeded in solving the problem for very long. Now the crucial question has become not how to stay alive but what to do with a life that is practically guaranteed.

The old professor was right: Too many of us do too little with it. Where will you find half the male population of the United States on any crisp Sunday afternoon in October or November? hunting? fishing? flying kites or model airplanes with the kids? roaming the russet fields, tramping the flaming woods? or sprawled in a darkened room watching twenty-two professional gladiators bang one another around on an electronic screen? By and large the silent watchers are faithful taxpayers and solid citizens. They will discuss with genuine concern such national problems as kidnapings, drug addiction, delinquency, crime. But which, really, is the more urgent issue of our time: the erratic, destructive, lawless behavior of the few or the ever-increasing inertia of the many?

The whole thing hangs on a series of decisions that each of us is constantly being called upon to make, decisions that spell the difference between living and nonliving. Often the margin is a narrow one, and it tends to grow even narrower as one grows older. But this is all the more reason for being everlastingly aware of the danger and on guard against it.

As a youngster I remember being given a solemn bit of advice that was supposed to apply to almost any situation: "When in doubt, don't." Well, perhaps this cautious approach has occasional value as a brake on the impetuousity of youth. But its usefulness diminishes rapidly once you're past twenty, it can be dangerously habit-forming after thirty, and after forty it probably should be reversed altogether, becoming: "When in doubt, do." If you can keep that formula in mind, the problems of nonliving are not likely to become much of a threat.

But they coil around many people today, and thoughtful observers are troubled. On my desk lies a letter from a friend, a clergyman. "The trouble with most of us," he writes, "isn't active or deliberate wickedness; it's lethargy, absence of caring, lack of involvement in life. To keep our bodies comfortable and well fed and entertained seems to be all that matters. But the more successful we are at this, the more entombed the soul becomes in solid, immovable flesh. We no longer hear the distant trumpet and go toward it; we listen to the pipes of Pan and fall asleep." And this good man goes on wistfully: "How can I rouse my people, make them yearn for something more than pleasant, socially acceptable ways of escaping from life? How can I make them want to thrust forward into the unknown, into the world of testing and trusting their own spirit? Oh, how I wish I knew!"

There's only one answer, really. Each of us must be willing, at least sometimes, to chop wood instead of sitting by the fire. Each of us must guard against the influences that lull and seduce us toward a state of nonliving. Each of us must fight his own fight against the betrayal of life that comes from refusing to live it.

Every day, for every one of us, some distant trumpet sounds. But never too faint or too far for our answer to be: "Wait! I'm coming!"

Freedom Is a Two-edged Sword

Last summer on the Fourth of July I found myself in a group listening to a short patriotic address. The speaker talked about the meaning of Independence Day. He spoke of the men who signed the Declaration, their courage, their dedication. He reminded us of our heritage of freedom, how precious it is, and how jealously we should guard it.

We applauded when he was through. But suddenly, as the applause died away, a voice spoke from the crowd: "Why don't you tell them the whole truth?"

Startled, we all looked around. The words had come from a young man in a tweed jacket with untidy hair and intense, angry eyes. He might have been a college student, a poet, a Peace Corps worker, almost anything.

"Why don't you tell them that freedom is the most dangerous gift anyone can receive?" he said. "Why don't you tell them that it's a two-edged sword that will destroy us unless we learn how to use it, and soon? Why don't you make them see that we face a greater challenge than our ancestors ever did? They only had to *fight* for freedom. We have to *live* with it!" He stared for a moment at our blank, uncomprehending faces. Then he shrugged his way through the crowd and was gone.

Now, almost a year later, I find myself still thinking about that young man. I think he was a person seized by a swift and stunning insight, and he had the courage to shout it out. He was right: Freedom *is* dangerous; it *can* be a two-edged blade. Look at this country today. All around us there seems to be a drastic decline in morals: cheating where once there was honesty, promiscuity where once there was decency, crime where once there was respect for law. Everywhere there seems to be a growing laxness, an indifference, a softness that terrifies people who think about it.

And what lies behind all this? Perhaps the angry young man was trying to tell us the truth. Perhaps we *do* have a blind and misguided concept of liberty. Perhaps we *are* using the freedom of choice gained for us by our forefathers to choose the wrong things.

Ever since our country won its independence, something in us has been deeply suspicious of authority. "Give us more freedom!" has been our constant cry. This was valid when it was directed against tyranny or oppression or exploitation, but we have pushed the concept far beyond that. The freedom we now claim has come to mean freedom from all unpleasantness: from hardship, from discipline, from the stern voice of duty, from the pain of self-sacrifice.

"Give us fewer rules, or more elastic ones!" This demand has weakened our courts of justice and shaken the foundations of the church.

"Give us more leisure and less work!" This one sounds enlightened and alluring, but at the end of the road lie sterility and boredom.

"Give us the freedom to decide moral questions for ourselves!" This one ignores the fact that once morals become relative it is hard to justify any morality at all.

As a nation, in short, we have clamored for total freedom. Now we have just about got it, and we are facing a bleak and chilling truth: We have flung off one external restraint after another, but in the process we have not learned how to restrain ourselves.

It is this truth that causes, deep in our souls, the uneasiness we feel despite all our prosperity and power. It is the knowledge that we have abandoned our ancient certainties but have so far found nothing to replace them. It is the premonition that unless we learn to control ourselves this climate of ultrafreedom may be replaced by a climate of repression. It is the fear that if we do not learn to guard and preserve our own best values, some form of tyranny will surely attempt to take them from us. This is no idle fear. It took Babylon 1000 years, and Rome 500, to decline and fall, but we have no such comfortable margin. Time and distance have diminished; the clock of history ticks faster.

So maybe on this Independence Day we should be thinking not so much about the freedom from tyranny that our ancestors won, as about the chaos that freedom can bring to those who do not use it wisely. We should ponder the truth of the old saying, "A man's worst difficulties begin when he is able to do what he likes." We should face up to the fact that, in the proportion to which we dismiss our external restraints, each of us has a solemn moral obligation to restrain himself.

This can never be easy. But the time has come in our national life when we need to look straight at some of the ugly areas in our society—the divorce statistics, the crime statistics, the weakening of family ties, the swirling clouds of racial hatred, the sex explosion on our campuses, the grim persistence of alcoholism, the death toll on our highways—and ask ourselves to what extent these things stem from a distorted concept of freedom which leaves men free to be selfish, free to be lazy, free to be ignoble, free to be weak.

If personal freedom of choice is our goal and our ideal as a nation, then our first and fundamental choice must be not to abuse that freedom. This is what independence really means: *self-discipline.* And this we would do well to remember when we see the flag we love blazing against the sky on Independence Day.

Enthusiasm—The Indwelling Deity

In the days when I was young, and fantasy was still in fashion, we used to hear a lot about fairy godmothers, amiable creatures who went around peering into cradles and casting all sorts of spells. With the wave of a wand, so we were told, they could endow a new baby with beauty, brains, courage, wealth, happiness—or almost anything.

This all seemed very satisfying, at the time. But now, looking back through the years, it seems to me that these fairy godmothers left out the most desirable quality of all. Not one that I can remember ever leaned close and whispered, "Lucky child, I bestow upon thee the gift of enthusiasm!"

Enthusiasm—from the beginning, a remarkable word. The ancient Greeks used it to describe an inspired person: *en* meaning in, and *theos* meaning god. The enthusiastic person, they thought, was one who reflected the presence of an in-dwelling god. And the more you ponder this, the more convinced you become that the Greeks, as usual, not only had a word for it, but the right word.

No other single human characteristic (with the possible exception of kindness) contributes so much to happy and successful living. Wise men have always known this. "Nothing great," said Emerson, "was ever achieved without enthusiasm." And yet, it's not a complicated or mysterious quality. You don't have to consult the sages to observe it or learn about it. Most children have it. So do good hunting dogs—that's why they're good.

What, exactly, is it? I would define it as the ability to react with eagerness. The enthusiastic person has the capacity for generating excitement about ideas, people, events —anything. He responds to the stimuli of life not only with his five senses and his brain, but with his emotions as well. He feels things. He *cares*. And in proportion as he cares, he is alive—just as when you stop caring altogether you are dead.

Enthusiasm is more than simple excitement, though. It also involves affection for the object that arouses it. The enthusiastic person loves the thing he feels excited about, great or small, important or unimportant, a marriage partner or an ice-cream cone. When he feels enthusiasm, he gives out love, and this—I'm sure—is the indwelling deity that the Greeks had in mind—or perhaps a fragment of the Kingdom of God that the Bible says is within us.

That is why the display of enthusiasm is such an endearing and contagious thing. We bring our children a ten-cent toy, or perhaps nothing but ourselves. "Hooray!" they cry, rushing pell-mell down the stairs as if all the riches of the world awaited them. What parent has not experienced this and felt the answering warmth in his own heart? Or, "It's a great day!" someone will say, for no particular reason, and at once we feel a strong impulse to agree with him.

Because it has optimism in it, because it's closely allied to cheerfulness, enthusiasm has the power to lift people over the rough places in life. Which of us does not admire some friend who has proved his capacity to endure staggering blows, keeping his sense of humor, his interest in things, his vitality intact? We marvel, as a rule, that such a person is able to retain his enthusiasm. The truth probably is that his enthusiasm—the love power inside—is supporting *him*.

Where does it come from, this love power, this capacity to react with gladness? I rather suspect that it is built into all of us, that each of us starts out in life with an adequate supply. Most young things, from colts to kittens, seem to be handsomely endowed with it. The problem is how to retain it once the freshness and eagerness of youth are past.

Certain inevitable aspects of living seem to be the enemy of enthusiasm. Routine deadens it, familiarity dulls it. From my window, as I write this, I can see a disdainful cat walking along the top of a fence. Just a plain alley cat, nothing to be excited about. But suppose I had never seen a cat before. Suppose this incredibly graceful creature was the *only* cat in existence. Imagine, then, the excitement he would cause, the price he would command!

A lot of people learned during the war how scarcity can sharpen perceptions and heighten enthusiasm. Once, flying home from blacked-out Britain, my plane landed briefly in Iceland, and somebody handed me an orange. I hadn't seen an orange for over a year, much less tasted one; but for a long time I couldn't bring myself to eat it. As we roared on to Greenland over the steel-gray sea, I sat there and stroked that orange and smelled it and held it up to the light to admire its color. In the end, I did eat it. It was sensational; I've never had an orange like that one since. I really loved that orange, and perhaps because I loved it I learned something from it.

I learned that sometimes, when you're feeling jaded or blasé, you can revive your sense of wonder by saying to yourself: *Suppose this were the only time. Suppose this sunset, this moonrise, this symphony, this buttered toast, this sleeping child, this flag against the sky . . . suppose you would never experience these things again!* An artificial device, perhaps, but for me it works. Few things are commonplace in themselves. It's our reaction to them that grows dull, as we move forward through the years.

This is not to say that one must be enthusiastic about

everything. Enthusiasm has to be selective, or it becomes fatuous. I always raise my eyebrows, mentally, when I hear someone claim that he is never bored. *Brother,* I say to myself, *you're in a bad way. What you're really claiming is that you have no discrimination at all!* Actually, boredom can be a useful emotion when it serves as a spur, when it impels people to action. Vitality, interest, curiosity, enthusiasm —these are the life manifestations. Apathy, indifference, inaction—these lead to inertia and finally to death.

The greatest Teacher who ever lived was well aware of these conflicting impulses in the human heart, and left no doubt as to which side He was on. *I am come,* He said, *that they might have life, and that they might have it more abundantly.* Small children, we are told, could not resist flinging themselves headlong upon Him. *Forbid them not,* He said, and He must have been smiling. *Of such is the kingdom of Heaven.* Most people think that He was referring to their artlessness and innocence, and maybe He was. I like to believe He also had in mind their energy and enthusiasm.

It has been said that the successful man is one who carries the best qualities of childhood into the later years. This is borne out by many of our famous contemporaries: They seem to retain the inquisitiveness, the wonder, the sense of freshness and discovery much longer than most of us. They take up new activities at any time, any stage of life. Their interests are highly varied. Consider Churchill with his painting, his writing, his bricklaying, his goldfish raising. Juliette Low, founder of the girl scouts in this country, was also a first-class artist and sculptress. More than that, when she wanted some gigantic wrought-iron gates for her home, she didn't go out and buy some. She got a blacksmith to teach her how to forge them herself.

Not all of us can be Churchills or Juliette Lows, but there is no reason why we can't recognize the importance of this indwelling god, and try to retain it in ourselves and encourage it in our children. One wonderful thing about enthusiasm is that is is so easy to kindle a blaze if the spark is there.

Not long ago, when our seven-year-old showed some interest, I bought her an illustrated book about astronomy. Ever since, she has been enthralled. She knows the order of the planets. She knows the size of Jupiter. She will tell you how many moons revolve around Mars. No doubt this intensity of interest will fade. But while it lasts there is an incandescence about it, a brightness that marks the presence of the indwelling god, the deity within.

Each of us has some of that divine spark, more perhaps than we know. Some of us let it grow dim under the dust of daily living. Some of us, like the man in the Parable of the Talents, hoard it jealously, bury it for safekeeping deep within ourselves. This is a mistake. Enthusiasm, like any other form of love power, needs to be expressed, must be liberated if it is to grow. People who give free rein to their enthusiasm will never run short of it, for by so doing they are constantly adding to the supply.

Enthusiasm: the greatest gift in the world! But to keep it, you have to give it away.

A Sharing of Wonder

Many summers ago a small boy lived in a tall house by the sea. The house had a tremendous peaked roof made of weathered shingles that towered above all the surrounding cottages. In this roof, near the top, was a trapdoor that could be reached only by a ladder propped up on the attic floor. Children used to play in the attic sometimes, but no one ever climbed up to the trapdoor. It was too high and forbidding.

One sunny day, however, when the boy's father was storing some boxes in the attic, he glanced up at the underside of the great roof. "Must be quite a view from up there," he said to his son. "Why don't we take a look?"

The boy felt his heart lurch with excitement and a touch of fear, but his father was already testing the shaky ladder. "Up you go," he said. "I'll be right behind you."

Up they went through the mysterious darkness, each step a terror and a delight. Up through the tiny sunbeams lancing through the cracks, up until the boy could smell the ancient heat-soaked shingles, up until the trapdoor, sealed with cobwebs, touched the top of his head. His father unhooked a latch, slid the trapdoor back . . . and a whole new universe burst upon his dazzled eyes.

There lay the sea—but what a sea! Gigantic, limitless, blazing with splintered sunlight, it curved away to infinity, dwarfing the land, rivaling the sky. Below him, queerly inverted, were the tops of trees and—even more unimaginable—the backs of gulls in flight. The familiar path through the dunes was a mere thread where heat waves shimmered; far away a shrunken river with toy boats coiled into the sea. All this he saw at a glance from the protective circle of his father's arm, and the impact of such newness, of such violently expanded horizons, was so great that from that moment the world of his childhood was somehow altered. It was stretched; it was different; it was never quite the same again.

Decades have passed since then; most of the minor trials and triumphs of childhood have faded from my mind. But I remember that moment on the roof as if it had happened yesterday. And I think of it sometimes when the day set aside as Father's Day comes round, because it seems to me that the real Father's Day is not this sentimentalized, over-commercialized occasion at all. The real Father's Day is the day that exists only in memory, in the mind of some happy child or nostalgic adult, the magical day when—just for a moment or perhaps simply by accident—a chord was struck, a spark jumped the gap between generations, a relationship was suddenly achieved so warm, so intense, that it was caught and held in the meshes of the mind, impervious to time.

My father has been dead for many years now, but he left so many Father's Days behind him that he doesn't seem to have gone very far. Whenever I want to feel close to him, all I have to do is choose one from the assortment in my mind labeled "the time we . . . ." Some are little-boy memories like the day on the roof; some are teen-age recollections; some no doubt would seem trivial to anyone else, but all have the same quality: a sense of exploration, a discovery of newness, a sharing of wonder.

There was the time we went to see a captured German U-boat that our navy had brought into the harbor. We climbed down into the maze of machinery smelling coldly of oil and war and claustrophobia and death. Another visitor asked my father bitterly if he did not consider the German sailors murderers who struck without warning from the depths of the sea. I remember how he shook his head, saying that they, too, were brave men caught like their adversaries in the iron trap of war. The answer did not please his questioner, but somehow brought relief and pride to me, as if a sudden test had been met and mastered.

Or the time we explored a cave, and at one point far underground snapped off our flashlights and sat there in darkness and silence so profound that it was like being in the void before the beginning of time. After a while Father said, in a whisper, "Listen! You can hear the mountain breathing!" And such is the power of suggestion that I did seem to hear, in the ringing silence, a tremendous rhythm that haunts me to this day.

Did my father deliberately set out to manufacture Father's Days for his children? I doubt it. In the episodes I remember so vividly I don't think he was primarily seeking to instruct or inspire or enlighten us. He was satisfying his own curiosity—and letting us in on his discoveries. He was indulging his own sense of wonder—and letting us share it.

This is the stuff of which *real* Father's Days—and Mother's Days also—are made. Sometimes, when the formula works, the parents may not even know it. But sometimes you do know, and when this happens there is no satisfaction in the world quite like it.

Not long ago our family visited one of those marine establishments where trained porpoises—and in this case a small whale—put on a marvelous show. I was so fascinated by the whale that I lingered after the performance to ask the trainer how it was captured, what it was fed, and so on. He was an obliging fellow who not only answered the questions but summoned the whale herself to the side of the pool. We patted her back, smooth and hard and gleaming like wet black rubber. This evidently pleased her, for suddenly she raised her great barrel of a head out of the water, rested it on the coping and gazed with friendly, reddish eyes at our eight-year-old daughter, who was nearest.

"Apparently," I said, "she wants to rub noses with you."

Our daughter looked both interested and aghast.

"Go ahead," the trainer said good-naturedly. "She won't mind."

There was an electric pause, then the briefest of damp contacts, then both participants hastily withdrew. And that seemed to be the end of it, until bedtime that night. Then, staring pensively at the ceiling, my daughter said, "Do you think any other third-grader in the whole wide world ever rubbed noses with a whale?"

"No," I said, "I'm pretty sure you're the only one."

She gave a deep, contented sigh, went to sleep, and hasn't mentioned it since. But thirty years from now, when her nose tingles, or when she touches wet black rubber, or sometimes for no reason at all, maybe . . . just maybe . . . she will remember.

7

The Gift
of Adaptability

Attitudes, a great American psychiatrist has said, are more important than facts. Maybe so. Certainly most of us spend our lives trying to improve our attitudes, shifting them, adjusting them, changing them as best we can to fit the changing realities that surround us.

In this endless effort, flexibility is the key to success—and a touch of humility, perhaps. The rigid person is the least likely to learn new thought-patterns, acquire new habits, experiment with new philosophies or life-styles. Self-satisfied people see no need to change themselves or their way of looking at things.

We writers (preachers or reformers at heart) are forever trying to tell people how to rearrange their personalities or reorder their lives. We sound very sure of ourselves, very Olympian, very grand.

But the truth is, most of the time we are preaching at ourselves.

Be Bold

Once when I was facing a decision that involved (I thought) considerable risk, I took the problem to a friend much older and wiser than myself. "I'd go ahead," I said unhappily, "if I were sure I could swing it. But . . . ."

He looked at me for a moment, then scribbled ten words on a piece of paper and pushed it across the desk. I picked it up and read, in a single sentence, the best advice I ever had: BE BOLD—AND MIGHTY FORCES WILL COME TO YOUR AID.

It's amazing how even a fragment of truth will illuminate things. The words my friend had written were from a quotation, I discovered later, from *The Conquest of Fear* by Basil King. They made me see clearly that in the past, whenever I had fallen short in almost any undertaking, it was seldom because I had tried and failed. It was because I had let fear of failure stop me from trying at all.

On the other hand, whenever I *had* plunged into deep water, impelled by a momentary flash of courage or just plain pushed by the rude hand of circumstance, I had always been able to swim until I got my feet on the ground again.

BE BOLD—that was no exhortation to be reckless or foolhardy. Boldness meant a deliberate decision, from time to time, to bite off more than you were sure you could chew. And there was nothing vague or mysterious about the mighty forces referred to. They were the latent powers that all of us possess: energy, skill, sound judgment, creative ideas—yes, even physical strength and endurance in far greater measure than most of us realize.

Boldness, in other words, creates a state of emergency to which the organism will respond. I once heard a famous British mountaineer say that occasionally a climber will get himself into a position where he can't back down, he can only go up. He added that sometimes he put himself into such a spot on purpose. "When there's nowhere to go but up," he said, "you jolly well go up!"

The same principle works, less dramatically but just as surely, in something as commonplace as accepting the chairmanship of some civic committee, or even seeking a more responsible job. In either case, you know you'll have to deliver—or else. And unless you're hopelessly unqualified, you *will* deliver. Your pride, your competitive instinct, and your sense of obligation will see to it that you do.

These are some of the mighty forces that will come to your aid. They are, admittedly, psychic forces. But they are more important than physical ones. It was centrifugal force, in a hurtling pebble, that killed Goliath. But it was courage that enabled David to face the champion of the Philistines in the first place.

It's curious, actually, how spiritual laws often have their counterpart in the physical world. A college classmate of mine was a crack football player, noted particularly for his fierce tackling although he was much lighter than the average varsity player. Someone remarked that it was surprising that he didn't get hurt.

"Well," he said, "I think it goes back to something I discovered when I was a somewhat timid youngster playing sandlot football. In one game, playing safety, I suddenly found myself confronting the opposing fullback, who had nothing but me between him and our goal line. He looked absolutely gigantic! I was so frightened that I closed my eyes and hurled myself at him like a panicky bullet—and stopped him cold. Right there I learned that the harder you tackle a bigger player, the less likely you are to be hurt. The reason is simple: Momentum equals weight times velocity."

In other words, if you are bold enough, even the laws of motion will come to your aid.

This personality trait—a willingness to put yourself in a position where you will have to extend yourself to the utmost—is not one that can be acquired overnight. But it can be taught to children and developed in adults. Confidence is a cumulative thing.

To be sure, there will be setbacks and disappointments in any program of expanded living; boldness in itself is no guarantee of success. But, as someone said, the man who tries to do something and fails is a lot better off than the man who tries to do nothing and succeeds.

Boldness, of course, like any other virtue, can be pushed too far. Once, in my more impulsive days, I jumped out of an airplane just to see what it was like. I had a parachute, naturally—two, in fact—but I promptly wound up in a hospital with a broken ankle. I suppose I did achieve my main objective, which was to write a story about paratroopers with a certain amount of realism. But it was hardly worth it.

Still, for every time you thus overshoot your target, there are a hundred times that you undershoot it. In the famous Parable of the Talents, the servant who buries his master's money in the ground is severely reprimanded for failing to do anything with it or take any risk. And the servant's answer is very significant. It could be summarized in three words: *I was afraid*.

Fear (the opposite of boldness) is the most paralyzing of all emotions. It can literally stiffen the muscles, as anyone knows who has ever been really scared. And (again the psychic-physical parallel holds) it can also stupefy the mind and the will. Most of us free-lance writers know this very well. When you are blessed—or cursed—with a vivid imagination, it's all too easy to become convinced that your energy is dwindling, that the flow of ideas is drying up, that your latest effort is also your last. Such thoughts are dangerous. Fears, like hopes and dreams, have a way of clothing themselves ultimately with reality. As Job said, reviewing his troubles (and anticipating the psychiatrists by a couple of millennia), "The thing which I greatly feared is come upon me . . . ."

Almost from the beginning of recorded history, mankind has recognized that the surest antidote for fear is religious faith. Belief—and trust—in a personal God makes a man bigger than himself and stronger than himself. Washington bore witness to this repeatedly; so did Lincoln. Joan of Arc was a shining example of the power of faith to transform an individual, and through an individual a whole nation.

This source of power is just as available to the rank and file as to the leaders. The man who believes firmly that the Creator of the universe loves him and cares infinitely what he does with his life—this man is automatically freed from much of the self-distrust that afflicts less certain men. Fear, guilt, hostility, anger—these are the emotions that stifle thought and impede action. By reducing or eliminating them, religious faith makes achievement possible. Over and over again, in both the Old and New Testaments, the Bible hammers this message home: *The Lord is my light and my salvation; whom shall I fear? . . . According to your faith be it unto you.*

Boldness is not always spectacular; there is also a quiet kind. I knew a city-dwelling family once that wanted to move to the country. They had no financial resources, but plenty of spiritual ones. Instead of counting the pennies and deciding the move was impossible, they calmly drew up a list of six requirements that they considered essential (actually, they agreed they would settle for five of the six). The place, they decided, would have to have a pleasant view, some shade trees, a stream or brook, some arable land to grow things, some pasture for animals, and it had to be near enough to the city for the father to milk the cows every morning and still commute to his job.

They finally found such a place, borrowed the money to make a down payment, and have been living there happily (and boldly, although no doubt the word would astonish them) ever since.

This sort of self-confidence and decisiveness often marks a leader in the business world. The best executive I ever worked for was a man who made almost instantaneous decisions. "At least," he used to say wryly, "I make my mistakes quickly." On one occasion someone asked this man if he didn't believe in the old adage, "Look before you leap."

"No," he said cheerfully, "I don't." He thought for a minute, then added, "The trouble with that axiom is that if you look too long, or too often, you never leap at all."

A willingness to take chances, a solid faith in the ability of the individual to cope, God helping him, with just about any problem—these characteristics are part of the traditional American heritage. Is that spirit dying out? Some observers claim that our preoccupation with security is weakening it. Initiative, they say, is the instinctive response to lack. Security is the absence of lack. Can the two really exist, side by side?

I think they can, simply because there are always new and more challenging worlds to conquer. We may be remembered as the generation that sought, and provided, material security for many. But we are also the generation that dared to pick the lock of the universe, the generation that invaded the heart of the atom. The risks were, and still are, appalling. But the mighty forces unleashed by our boldness will come to our aid some day in the form of unlimited light and heat and power for all mankind.

One of the best speeches I ever heard was made by a little man who came into our schoolroom one day and was invited to say a few words to us. I don't remember who he was and probably I am not quoting him verbatim, but what he said was very close to this:

> Love life. Be grateful for it always. And show your gratitude by not shying away from its challenges. Try always to live a little bit beyond your capacities. You'll find that you never succeed.

Know the Right Moment

I shall never forget an interview I had with that grand old actor Charles Coburn. I asked a stock question: What does one need to get ahead in life? Brains? Energy? Education?

He shook his head. "Those things help. But there's something I consider even more important: *knowing the moment.*"

I remember staring at him, pencil poised. "What moment?"

"The moment," he said, "to act—or not to act. The moment to speak—or to keep silent. On the stage, as every actor knows, timing is the all-important factor. I believe it's the key in life, too. If you master the art of knowing the moment, in your marriage, your work, your relationship with others, you won't have to pursue happiness and success. They'll walk right in through your front door!"

The old actor was right. If you can learn to recognize the right moment when it comes, and act before it goes away, the problems of life become vastly simplified. People who repeatedly meet with failure are often disheartened by what seems to be a relentlessly hostile world. What they almost never realize is that time and again they are making the right effort—but at the wrong moment. "Oh, these quarreling couples," I heard a family-relations-court judge say the other day. "If only they'd realize that there are times when everyone's threshold of irritability is low, when a person can't stand nagging or criticism—or even good advice! If married partners would just take the trouble to study each other's moods, and know when to air a grievance or when to show affection, the divorce rate in this country would be cut in half!"

The judge was saying what Charles Coburn had said: Know the moment. Once, in a penitent mood, I asked my wife which of my smaller failings annoyed her most. "Your tendency," she said promptly, "to wait until we're about to walk into a party before telling me that my hair is mussed or my dress doesn't look quite right."

Good manners are often nothing but good timing. What is more annoying than to be interrupted in mid-anecdote? Who has not been trapped for what seems a lifetime by the bore who never knows when to leave?

Good timing sometimes means doing the unexpected. Down in Georgia a doctor who had arranged for a childless couple to adopt a baby was making some late night calls with his wife. Suddenly he said, "The adoption papers are all in order. Let's go to the hospital and get the baby for Ruth and Kenneth."

"At this hour?" cried his wife. "Why, they're not supposed to get the baby for several days. They'd be scared to death!"

"Ha!" said the doctor. "New babies have a way of arriving late at night—and first-time parents are always scared to death. It'll give them a good, normal start. Let's do it!"

So the baby was "delivered" in the middle of the night; the parents were flustered and excited, and it was indeed a memorable beginning.

For a long time I thought that timing was a gift, something you were born with, like an ear for music. But gradually, observing people who seemed blessed with the gift, I realized it was a skill that could be acquired by anyone who cared to make the effort. To master the art of good timing, keep five requirements in mind:

First, keep yourself constantly aware of how decisive timing can be in human affairs, of how true Shakespeare's insight was when he wrote, "There is a tide in the affairs of men which, taken at the flood, leads on to fortune." Once you have grasped the full importance of "knowing the moment," you have taken the first step toward acquiring a capacity for it.

Next, make a pact with yourself (a pact you will undoubtedly break at times) *never to act or speak when driven by the whirlwinds of anger, fear, hurt, jealousy, or resentment.* These emotional monkey wrenches can wreck the most carefully developed timing mechanism. At a turbulent public meeting once I lost my temper and said some harsh and sarcastic things. The proposal I was supporting was promptly defeated. My father, who was there, said nothing, but that night, on my pillow, I found a marked passage from Aristotle: "Anybody can become angry—that is easy; but to be angry with the right person, and to the right degree, and at the right time, and for the right purpose, and in the right way—that is not within everybody's power and is not easy."

Third, sharpen your powers of anticipation. The future is not a closed book. Much of what is going to happen is determined by what is happening now. Yet relatively few people make a conscious effort to project themselves beyond the present, gauge future probabilities, and act accordingly.

This look-ahead capacity is so important in business that many corporations make it a main yardstick for job advancement. But it is just as important in running a household. Will Saturday be a good day for a trip to the beach? Better have cold cuts and sandwich bread on hand just in case. Is your widowed mother-in-law's health beginning to fail? Better face the possibility that she may have to move in with you or be placed in a nursing home. The art of good timing includes knowing the moment when present action will eliminate future trouble or gain future advantages.

Fourth, learn patience. You just have to believe, with Emerson, that "if the single man plant himself indomitably on his instincts, and there abide, the huge world will come round to him." There is no easy formula for acquiring patience; it is a subtle blend of wisdom and self-control. But one must learn that premature action can often spoil everything.

The final—and most difficult—step is *learning to get outside yourself.* Each moment is shared by every living creature, but each person sees it from a different point of view. Really knowing the moment, then, includes knowing how it looks to other people.

A great philanthropist, the late Mrs. John Dibert of New Orleans, told how one night in midwinter, as she was riffling through a magazine, her eyes were caught by a cartoon. In it, two ragged old women were shivering over a meager fire. "What you thinkin' about?" asked one. "About the nice warm clothes the rich ladies will be giving us next summer," answered the other.

Mrs. Dibert, supporter of hospitals, donor to many charities, looked at the cartoon for a long time. Finally she went up into the attic, unpacked trunks, made bundles of warm clothes to be distributed the next day. She resolved to time her charity better, to give, as she put it, "to the ones whose needs are *now.*"

As the Old Testament says:

To every thing there is a season, and a time to every purpose under the heaven.

The Power in Purposeful Pausing

A few years ago, on a liner bound for Europe, I was browsing in the library when I came across a puzzling line by Robert Louis Stevenson: "Extreme busyness, whether at school, kirk or market, is a symptom of deficient vitality." Surely, I thought, "deficient" is a mistake—he must have meant "abundant." But R.L.S. went merrily on, "It is no good speaking to such folk: they *can not* be idle, their nature is not generous enough."

Was it possible that a bustling display of energy might only be camouflage for a spiritual vacuum? The thought so impressed me that I mentioned it next day to the French purser, at whose table I was sitting. He nodded his agreement. "Stevenson is right," he said. "Indeed, if you will pardon my saying so, the idea applies particularly to you Americans. A lot of your countrymen keep so busy getting things done that they reach the end of their lives without ever having lived at all."

On the other side of me was a fragile little Chinese scholar from Hong Kong. "True," he said. "When there is no time for quiet, there is no time for the soul to grow. The man who walks through a countryside sees much more than the man who runs." He smiled and waved a fine-boned hand. "Sometimes, when you have a task to do, try doing it tomorrow instead of today. In the end, maybe you will get more done—because maybe you will live longer!"

It was advice that sounded like heresy to me. I had crammed my life full, prided myself on never having an idle moment. But now I began to experiment with a little purposeful pausing. And slowly I began to see that this change of pace actually enhanced the excitement of living. I slowed myself down to the point where a breathless awareness of everything gave way to a truer appreciation of essentials: The landscape ceased to be a blur and became a countryside with detail, color, dimension, and depth.

One surprising discovery was that pausing can increase efficiency. I found that if you deliberately put off a task for a day or two, you are often likely to do it better. For one thing, waiting sometimes dispels the tension that results from an imagined urgency, and so you make fewer mistakes. For another, when you get around to working on the problem, often you find that certain elements of it are already solved by your subconscious mind.

Another advantage of pausing is that it gives you a better chance to make a decision that is morally right. A central figure in a celebrated scandal was quoted recently as saying, "All my life I've been in a hurry." The remark is significant. He was hurrying so fast that he had no time to read the signposts on the boundary that divides honesty from dishonesty.

Still another discovery I made was that leisureliness, tranquility, little periods of deliberate aimlessness—these things draw people together. Fishermen know this sort of comradeship well. But you don't have to be a fisherman to achieve it. Try spending an hour with your husband or wife just sauntering along the street, window-shopping. Or hunt for pinecones or mushrooms in a wood with the children (children are instinctive pausers). The ancient prohibition against work and organized entertainment on Sunday was designed to create this atmosphere of spiritual harmony. When you practice the art of pausing, you are really scattering fragments of Sunday throughout the week.

In the last few years, industry has learned the value of coffee breaks: Production is higher when work is interrupted briefly. Many top executives now give themselves a half hour after lunch when they take no phone calls. One man I know, whenever he's faced with an endless series of visitors, arranges for a three-minute interval between appointments. He leans back, puts his feet on the desk and stares out the window. If his mind goes blank, so much the better—it will be all the fresher when the next visitor comes in.

Anyone who will step back and take a look at his way of life can find ways to slow down without resorting to tranquilizers. Why shouldn't the busy housewife, between chores, kick off her shoes, lie down on the sofa, and daydream for a few minutes? If her conscience tries to intrude, it should be sent on an errand. When she gets up she'll find that a lot of energy has flowed back into her.

Pausers are not time-wasters; they are time-*users*. Thoreau's solitary reflections around Walden Pond produced the insights that made him famous. It was Thoreau who said, "The swiftest traveler is he that goes afoot"—a remark that might well be the creative pauser's motto.

To be sure, pausing can be overdone. Lying in bed that extra five minutes is delightful; an extra hour might be not only dull but disastrous. Sooner or later most of us have to get up, go to the office, or get the children off to school, attend to the endless mechanics of living. But we will do these things better if we have the emotional balance and the controlled energy that come from deliberate slowing of the pace.

Why not try it? All it takes is a little *won't* power. Make up your mind that you won't be hurried, you won't be rushed, you won't—necessarily—do it now.

The Neglected Art of Being Different

One of the most vivid and painful recollections of my life concerns . . . a hat.

When I was eleven, my parents sent me to a summer camp run along semimilitary lines. Part of each camper's uniform was supposed to be a boy-scout hat, low-crowned, wide-brimmed, to be worn every afternoon without fail when we lined up for formal inspection.

But my parents did not provide me with a scout hat. Through some catastrophic oversight, they sent me off with one of those army campaign hats, vintage of 1917. It was wide-brimmed, all right: when I put it on, I was practically in total darkness. As for the crown, instead of being flat, it seemed to me to rise half a mile straight up in the air. Whenever I wore this hat, instead of being an inconspicuous and somewhat homesick small boy, I became a freak.

Or so I thought. Looking back now, across the years, I can smile at the memory of my wan little face peering out forlornly from under that monstrosity of a hat. But it was no joke at the time. I was miserable—utterly, abjectly miserable. Why? Because I was *different*, different from the others, different from the crowd.

There must be few of us who cannot recall from some such childhood episode the loneliness and terror of being different. And fewer still who do not carry some of this deep-rooted fear into adult life. It's a fear as fundamental as the fear of falling, and in a sense it *is* a fear of falling—of falling out of favor with other people by differing from them. But if we value leadership, if we prize achievement, if we are concerned with our own painful struggle toward maturity, we have to learn to overcome this fear, or at least to control it.

The rewards of differentness are easy enough to see. No matter what field you choose—science, entertainment, law, education, the business world—the demand is for individuals whose performance is above average and therefore different. At any dinner party, the liveliest and most attractive guest is the one whose ideas and observations are stimulating because they are different. I have no doubt that if a survey were made, the earning power of any given person would be found to parallel almost exactly his capacity to produce new ideas, to show unusual persistence or energy, to take chances—in other words, to be different.

The fear of being different, like most fears, tends to diminish when you drag it into the light and take a good look at it. At the bottom of such fear lies an intense preoccupation with self. That comical hat, back in my childhood, might have caused some momentary merriment or temporary teasing. But the whole thing was too trivial to have lasted long. I was the one who kept it alive by agonizing about it. Recognize this sort of self-consciousness as a form of inverted egotism, and you are not so likely to be victimized by it.

It also helps to remind yourself occasionally that some of the disapproval or hostility that you shrink from encountering is probably imaginary. This tendency to see menace where none exists afflicts us all, to some extent, and certainly begins early. We had a classic example, the other day, in our backyard. A visiting four-year-old encountered a small but lively cricket and yelled for help in piercing tones.

Our own three-year-old was very scornful about the whole thing. "Crickets don't hurt anybody," she said loftily. "I like crickets."

But the visitor was not to be cheated out of her fear so easily. "Crickets," she said with gloomy conviction, "don't like *me!*"

Another way to minimize the fear of being different is to remind yourself, if you really do run into resentment or ridicule, that you are in pretty good company. Very few of the great pioneers of thought or action escaped being laughed at, criticized, or even martyred.

Most of the great religious leaders of history have been nonconformists. Christ was a religious revolutionist. He defied authority, as when He healed sick people on the sabbath. He upset convention, as when He sat down to dinner with publicans and sinners. He was not afraid to use violence, as when He drove the money changers out of the temple.

It takes courage to be different, but there is also an art to it, the art of not antagonizing people unnecessarily by your differentness. People don't object to differentness nearly so much as they object to the attitude of superiority that so often goes with it.

Some very rugged individualists never learn this lesson. Half a century ago, Billy Mitchell's concept of air power was prophetic—and correct. Unfortunately, he could not conceal his conviction that anyone who disagreed with him was a fool. As a result, his hopes and dreams were thwarted for years; he didn't live to see their fulfillment.

The rule of thumb is very simple: Be as different as you like, but try to be tolerant of the people who differ from you. If we all granted to one another the right simply to be ourselves, we would be different enough. When he was eight years old, someone asked Henry Thoreau what he was going to be when he grew up. "Why," said the boy, "I will be I!" He was, too.

So take a look at your life and check the areas where you are letting a foolish fear of "what people might say" hold you down or hold you back. Then go ahead and do a few of these unorthodox things. The penalties will certainly be less—and the rewards may be much greater—than you think.

Minimaxims for My Godson

Dear Sandy,

Your nice thank-you note for the graduation present I sent you a few weeks ago just came in, and I've been chuckling over your postscript in which you say that such presents are dandy but you wish someone could give you "half a dozen foolproof ideas for bending the world into a pretzel."

Well, Sandy, I must admit I don't have any very original thoughts of my own. But through the years I've encountered a few ideas of that kind—not platitudes but ideas sharp-pointed enough to stick in my mind permanently. Concepts that release energy, make problem-solving easier, provide shortcuts to worthwhile goals. No one handed them over in a neat package. They just came along from time to time, usually from people not in the wisdom-dispensing business at all. Compared to the great time-tested codes of conduct, they may seem like pretty small change. But each of them has helped to make my life a good deal easier and happier and more productive.

So here they are. I hope you find them useful, too.

1. *If you can't change facts, try bending your attitudes.* Without doubt, the bleakest period of my life so far was the winter of 1942–43. I was with the Eighth Air Force in England. Our bomber bases, hacked out of the sodden English countryside, were seas of mud. On the ground, people were cold, miserable, homesick. In the air, people were getting shot. Replacements were few, morale was low.

But there was one sergeant—a crew chief—who was always cheerful, always good-humored, always smiling. I watched him one day, in a freezing rain, struggle to salvage a Fortress that had skidded off the runway into an apparently bottomless mire. He was whistling like a lark. "Sergeant," I said to him sourly, "how can you whistle in a mess like this?"

He gave me a mud-caked grin. "Lieutenant," he said, "when the facts won't budge, you have to bend your attitudes to fit them, that's all."

Check it for yourself, Sandy. You'll see that, faced with a given set of problems, one man may tackle them with intelligence, grace, and courage; another may react with resentment and bitterness; a third may run away altogether. In any life, facts tend to remain unyielding. But attitudes are a matter of choice—and that choice is largely up to you.

2. *Don't come up to the net behind nothing.* One night in a PTA meeting, a lawyer—a friend and frequent tennis partner of mine—made a proposal which I disagreed with and challenged. But when I had concluded what I thought was quite a good spur-of-the-moment argument, my friend stood up and proceeded to demolish it. Where I had had opinions, he had facts; where I had had theories, he had statistics. He obviously knew so much more about the subject than I did that his viewpoint easily prevailed. When we met in the hall afterward, he winked and said, "You should know better than to come up to the net behind nothing!"

It is true, the tennis player who follows his own weak or badly placed shot up to the net is hopelessly vulnerable. And this is true when you rush into *anything* without adequate preparation or planning. In any important endeavor, you've got to do your homework, get your facts straight, sharpen your skills. In other words, don't bluff—because if you do, nine times out of ten, life will drill a backhand right past you.

3. *When the ball is over, take off your dancing shoes.* As a child, I used to hear my aunt say this, and it puzzled me a good deal,

until the day I heard her spell out the lesson more explicitly. My sister had come back from a glamorous weekend full of glitter, exciting parties, and stimulating people. She was bemoaning the contrast with her routine job, her modest apartment, her day-to-day friends. "Young lady," our aunt said gently, "no one lives on the top of the mountain. It's fine to go there occasionally—for inspiration, for new perspectives. But you have to come down. Life is lived in the valleys. That's where the farms and gardens and orchards are, and where the plowing and the work are done. That's where you apply the visions you may have glimpsed from the peaks."

It's a steadying thought when the time comes, as it always does, to exchange your dancing shoes for your working shoes.

4. *Shine up your neighbor's halo.* One Sunday morning, drowsing in a back pew of a little country church, I dimly heard the old preacher urge his flock to "stop worrying about your own halo and shine up your neighbor's!" And it left me sitting up, wide-awake, because it struck me as just about the best eleven-word formula for getting along with people that I ever heard.

I like it for its implication that everyone, in some area of life, has a a halo that's worth watching for and acknowledging. I like it for the droll celestial picture it conjures up: Everybody industriously polishing away at everybody else's little circle of divine light. I like it for the firm way it shifts the emphasis from self to interest and concern for others. Finally, I like it because it reflects a deep psychological truth: People have a tendency to become what you expect them to be.

5. *Keep one eye on the law of the echo.* I remember very well the occasion when I heard this sharp-edged bit of advice. Coming home from boarding school, some of us youngsters were in the dining car of a train. Somehow the talk got around to the subject of cheating on exams, and one boy

readily admitted that he cheated all the time. He said that he found it both easy and profitable.

Suddenly a mild-looking man sitting all alone at a table across the aisle—he might have been a banker, a bookkeeper, anything—leaned forward and spoke up. "Yes," he said directly to the apostle of cheating, "all the same—I'd keep one eye on the law of the echo, if I were you."

The law of the echo—is there really such a thing? Is the universe actually arranged so that whatever you send out —honesty or dishonesty, kindness or cruelty—ultimately comes back to you? It's hard to be sure. And yet, since the beginning of recorded history, mankind has had the conviction, based partly on intuition, partly on observation, that in the long run a man does indeed reap what he sows.

You know as well as I do, Sandy, that in this misty area there are no final answers. Still, as the man said, I think I'd keep one eye on the law of the echo, if I were you!

6. *Don't wear your raincoat in the shower.* In the distant days when I was a boy scout, I had a troop leader who was an ardent woodsman and naturalist. He would take us on hikes not saying a word, and then challenge us to describe what we had observed: trees, plants, birds, wildlife, everything. Invariably we hadn't seen a quarter as much as he had, nor half enough to satisfy him. "Creation is all around you," he would cry, waving his arms in vast inclusive circles. "But you're keeping it out. Don't be a buttoned-up person! Stop wearing your raincoat in the shower!"

I've never forgotten the ludicrous image of a person standing in a shower bath with a raincoat buttoned up to his chin. It was a memorable exhortation to heightened awareness.

The best way to discard that raincoat, I've found, is to expose yourself to new experiences. It's routine that dulls the eye and deadens the ear; novelty sharpens both. So if you want a heightened sense of fun, of excitement, of expectancy in your life, don't be a buttoned-up person. Get rid of that raincoat and let creation in!

All these phrases that I have been recalling really urge one to the same goal: a stronger participation, a deeper involvement in life. This doesn't come naturally, by any means. And yet, with marvelous impartiality, each of us is given exactly the same number of minutes and hours in every day. Time is the raw material. What we do with it is up to us.

A wise man once said that tragedy is not what we suffer, but what we miss. Keep that in mind, Sandy.

Your affectionate

GODFATHER

A Foolproof Formula for Success

When I was asked to give the commencement address at a nearby college, a friend said to me, "It's easy. All you have to do is give 'em a foolproof formula for success!"

It was said jokingly, but the remark stuck in my mind. And the more I thought about it, the more convinced I became that there *is* a foolproof formula for success, available to anyone wise enough to recognize it and put it to work.

In American industry the competition for promising personnel is terrific. Year after year businessmen study college records, screen applicants, and offer special inducements to proven people. What are they after, really? brains? energy? know-how? These things are desirable, sure. But they will carry a man only so far. If he's to move to the top and be entrusted with command decisions, there must be a plus factor, something that takes mere ability and doubles or trebles its effectiveness. To describe this magic characteristic there's only one word: *integrity*.

Basically, the word means *wholeness*. In mathematics, an integer is a number that isn't divided into fractions. Just so, a man of integrity isn't divided against himself. He doesn't think one thing and say another—so it's virtually impossible for him to lie. He doesn't believe in one thing and do another—so he's not in conflict with his own principles. It's the absence of inner warfare, I'm convinced, that gives a man the extra energy and clarity of thought that make achievement inevitable.

Integrity really means having a certain built-in set of attitudes. Let me give you examples.

Integrity means living up to the best in yourself. Years ago, a writer who had lost a fortune in bad investments went into bankruptcy. His intention was to pay off every cent he owed, and three years later he was still working at it. To help him, a newspaper organized a fund. Important people contributed heavily to it. It was a temptation—accepting would have meant the end of a wearing burden. But Mark Twain refused, and returned the money to the contributors. Seven months later, with his new book a hit, he paid the last of his debts in full.

Integrity means having a highly developed sense of honor. Not just honesty, mind you, *honor.* The great Frank Lloyd Wright once spoke of this to the American Institute of Architects. "What," he asked, "might this sense of honor be? Well, what is the honor of a brick; what would be an honorable brick? A *brick* brick, wouldn't it? What would be the honor of a board? It would be a good board, wouldn't it? What is the honor of man? To be a true individual." And that's exactly what Frank Lloyd Wright was: an individual true to his own standards and hence to himself.

Integrity means having a conscience and listening to it. "It is neither safe nor prudent," said Martin Luther, facing his enemies in the city where his death had been decreed, "to do aught against conscience. Here I stand; God help me, I cannot do otherwise."

Integrity means having the courage of your convictions. This includes the capacity to cling to what you think is right, to go it alone when necessary, and to speak out against what you know is wrong. In the operating room of a great hospital a young nurse had her first day of full responsibility. "You've removed eleven sponges, doctor," she said to the surgeon. "We used twelve."

"I've removed them all," the doctor declared. "We'll close the incision now."

"No," the nurse objected. "We used twelve."

"I'll take the responsibility," the surgeon said grimly. "Suture!"

"You can't do that!" blazed the nurse. "Think of the patient!"

The doctor smiled, lifted his foot, showed the nurse the twelfth sponge. "You'll do," he said. He had been testing her for integrity—and she had it.

Integrity means obedience to the unenforceable. In a way, this is the heart of it. No one can *force* you to live up to the best in yourself. No one can *compel* you to get involved. No one can *make* you obey your conscience. A person of integrity does these things anyway.

During World War II, when our armies were slashing across France, an American colonel and his jeep driver took a wrong turn and ran into an oncoming German armored column. Both men jumped out and took cover, the sergeant in some roadside bushes, the colonel in a culvert under the road. The Germans spotted the sergeant and advanced on him, firing. The colonel could easily have remained undetected. He chose, instead, to come out fighting—one pistol against tanks and machine guns. He was killed. The sergeant, taken prisoner, told the story later. Why did the colonel do it? Because his concept of duty, though unenforceable, was stronger than his regard for his own safety.

Difficult? Yes. That is why true integrity is rare, and admired. But in terms of ultimate reward it's worth all the effort. Just consider a few of the dividends that integrity pays:

Boldness. Integrity gives a person the strength to take chances, welcome challenge, reject the unsatisfactory-but-safe for the unknown-with-chance-for-improvement. A person of integrity has confidence and can believe in himself —because he has no reason to distrust himself.

Persistence. Integrity often shows up as an unshakable single-mindedness of purpose, a tenacity that refuses to give up. "Never give in!" said Winston Churchill. "Never, never, never, never. In nothing great or small, large or petty —never give in except to convictions of honor and good sense." And he never did.

Serenity. People of integrity, I've noticed, are shock-resistant. They seem to have a kind of built-in equanimity that enables them to accept setbacks, or even injustices. Harry Emerson Fosdick tells how Abraham Lincoln was warned by his friends not to make a certain speech while campaigning for the U.S. Senate in 1858. Lincoln replied, "If it is decreed that I should go down because of this speech, then let me go down linked to the truth." He was serene. He did go down, but two years later he became president.

There are many other benefits that integrity brings a person: friendship, trust, admiration, respect. One of the hopeful things about the human race is that people seem to recognize integrity almost instinctively—and are irresistibly attracted to it.

How does one acquire it? I'm sure there's no pat answer. I think perhaps the first step is schooling yourself to practice total honesty in little things: not telling that small lie when it's inconvenient to tell the truth; not repeating that juicy bit of gossip that is quite possibly untrue; not charging that personal phone call to the office.

Such discipline may sound small, but when you really seek integrity and begin to find it, it develops its own power that sweeps you along. Finally you begin to see that almost anything worth having has an integrity of its own that must not be violated.

A foolproof formula for success? Yes. It's foolproof because—*regardless of fame, money, power or any of the conventional yardstick*—if you seek and find integrity, you *are* a success.

Welcome to Danger

All through the bright month of June, all over this bright land of ours, class after graduating class of young Americans will be taking one of the most important steps of their lives—the long step from preparation to performance. On a golden afternoon or a lilac-scented evening, someone hands them a piece of paper or a parchment scroll. In that moment they pass from the pleasant world of the possible to the demanding world of the actual.

What should we say to these young people, we battle-weary members of an older generation? Should we congratulate them on being born into the richest nation in the world, on sharing the great adventures of the space age? Should we tell them how to be popular, or how to succeed in business without really trying?

I don't think so. I think we should tell them the truth. I think we should tell them what they're getting into, and what we need from them, and why.

I think we should say to them:

Members of the Graduating Class, welcome to trouble. And uncertainty. And danger. Our nation is prosperous and powerful, it's true. But it is also a beleaguered fortress in a hostile world. We have far more enemies than friends on this troubled planet. Even the envious neutrals do not wish us well.

Wherever you look, without or within, our problems are gigantic. The generation just ahead of you has fought three wars against external aggression; it has struggled with staggering internal problems of economics and social justice. We have done the best we could, and not too badly, perhaps, but in the process we have neglected some things.

What is your generation going to do about the steady rise of crime and delinquency? About the prevalence of payola and classroom cheating? About the sadism on television and the pornography in books and the preoccupation with perversion in our theaters?

Make no mistake about it, these are the classic and historic signs of decadence, of decay. And what is the answer? The answer is people. Not just any people. A special kind of people.

We need people who are *honest,* honest with the fierce intolerance that considers a lie contemptible and a broken promise a black disgrace.

We need people who are *intelligent,* people who can gauge probabilities, make judgments, take action. Already nations are seeking frantically to acquire the best brains of other nations. Intelligence, not yellow metal, is the gold standard of the future.

We need people who are *bold,* who are stimulated, not paralyzed, by danger, who can take the calculated risk and lose, if necessary; lose everything but the willingness to take the risk again.

We need people who are *patient,* but who can become dangerous if pushed too far. There is a point where tolerance ends and spinelessness begins. History speaks plainly about this: No nation ever won freedom without fighting for it, or kept it without being willing to fight.

We need people with a *passion for work,* not just for fame or money or security, but because of the satisfactions that come from achieving the difficult, or even attempting the impossible.

We need people who are *patriotic*, not with the blind conceit that can see no good in other nations, but with an awareness that love of country is essential to all people, because in pride there is confidence, and in confidence, achievement.

We need *cheerful*, warm people, people who love life, and know that it brings change, and welcome this. We need people with the imagination and humor and curiosity and love of the beautiful that transcend national boundaries and make them citizens of the world.

And where do such people come from? They come out of the heart and soul of any nation that remains capable of judging itself, of shrugging off its lunatic fringes, of demanding sacrifices when necessary, of insisting that its citizens keep trying to be better people than they are.

Such people come from homes where unselfishness is the cardinal rule of living; from schools where the basic discipline is self-discipline; from colleges whose concept of education involves not just the acquisition of knowledge, but a kind of endless pilgrimage toward the distant and difficult goals of justice, and honor, and service to mankind.

Since this country was founded, every generation has had its quota of such people. That is why our star has kept rising. Your generation will produce them, too, but there must be more than ever before, because the tides of history run faster and the need is greater than ever before.

Members of the Graduating Class, freedom is not just a privilege; it is a test, and those who cannot pass the test will be denied it. Welcome, then, to the proving grounds. Bring with you all the courage and vitality and determination you can muster.

You are going to need them, just as your country is going to need you.

8

The Gift
of Life—and Beyond

This whole book has been about the greatest of all gifts—life itself. Most of the time most of us take it for granted. We wake up every morning manifestly *here*. We walk, talk, sleep, eat, love, hate, and do everything else without considering the fact that, but for an almost random collision of cells nine months before our first breath, such awareness might never have been ours at all.

Nor do we like to think much about the day when such awareness will cease to be.

It has always seemed to me that living life is like being given free tickets to a marvelous play. Every day the curtain rises on a new scene, exhilarating and exciting. But, exciting though it is, this succession of scenes can't go on forever—which is probably just as well. Sooner or later even the most enthusiastic playgoer would grow weary and bored. No one—however thrilling the play —wants to stay in the theater all night.

What happens when one leaves the theater? You can believe, if you like, that nothing happens, that everything is as blank and dark as it was before the play started; or you can believe that some new form of awareness begins. You can believe anything you like. But you can never positively know.

As I grow older, I find myself tending to believe more and more that something does happen after death. The reason may seem weak or naïve to some people, but it carries considerable weight with me, and it is simply this: The whole thing—the whole vast tapestry of reality as we perceive it—the starry universe—the whirling masses of electrons that make up the Milky Way or the leaves on a tree—the trillions of cells that comprise my brain and the brains of countless other living creatures—the whole stupendous show—the whole unbelievable ball of wax—is just too complicated, too purposeful, too beautifully balanced, too cunningly arranged for all of it to end in meaninglessness. I find it harder and harder to believe that the entity we call a human being (and it seems more and more obvious to me that such an entity is a combination of thought and matter, or of the spiritual and the material if you like) simply ceases to exist after a change that removes the physical aspects of that entity.

I mean, *it's all just too complex to be pointless!*

Of course, this feeling may be nothing but pure egotism—man's eternal reluctance to relinquish his desperately needed sense of self-importance. As one minister I know likes to say, we don't try to prove immortality so that we can believe it; we try to prove it because we can't help believing it.

Maybe so. But whatever the reason, I think the chances of something being out there in that "undiscover'd country," as Shakespeare called it, are better than the chances of nothing being out there.

So that's where I stand on that.

Not many of the things I've written deal with death directly, because most editors feel (maybe rightly, maybe not) that readers are afraid of the subject, or at least find it depressing. But once or twice I have been steered toward the subject, not away from it.

Once this happened in England when Michael Randolph, editor of the British edition of the *Digest,* asked me to visit and report on a certain hospital on the edge of London. He said it would be a difficult assignment—and in a way it was. But it was also reassuring and rewarding.

The other time was when something happened in my own life and my American *Digest* editor John Allen urged me to set it down just as it occurred, adding nothing and subtracting nothing. I hesitated for a while, but finally I did.

I called that first effort "The End of the Journey." I called the second "Gone Home." But for Michael and John, neither of them could have been written.

Here they are.

The End of the Journey

The extraordinary thing was the absence of fear. Some hospitals are saturated with anxiety and loneliness. Here, in a place that specialized in terminal illness, I could sense none. Wards and private rooms in this medical foundation on the edge of London were bright with sunlight and flowers. In a room with greeting cards strung gaily above the bed, an attractive woman in her forties told me that her musician husband was opening that night in Copenhagen in *The Magic Flute*. "I'd love to be there," she said a bit wistfully. Then she added, matter-of-factly, "Perhaps if there's a London performance later on I'll make that."

In one of the small wards, a pair of elderly ladies joked with me, then both of them burst into peals of laughter, bringing smiles from everyone. Other patients, too, were alert and cheerful, whether in bed, or moving about, or chatting with visitors. *They aren't afraid or worried,* I said to myself; *you can see it in their faces.* Even the visitors looked relaxed, although they knew, as I did, that most of these patients would not be going home again.

I was on my way to an interview with the medical director, a woman doctor whose approach to the problem of death was said to be studied and admired by medical people throughout the world. I wanted to do an objective job of reporting, but there was also another reason. I had never looked squarely at this inevitability from which all of us are separated only by a thin barrier of time. If this doctor's philosophy and her handling of the reality of death could calm the fears that surround the subject, I wanted to know about them.

In her white coat she faced me across her desk. Her eyes were concerned, and I knew that the last thing she wanted was personal publicity, or any sensational or sentimental reporting of her work.

"We call ourselves a Hospice," she said, "because originally a hospice was a resting place for pilgrims, weary travelers who needed shelter. Most of the people who come to us are very tired. Some are lonely, many are frightened, a few are close to despair. The first thing we try to do is make them feel at home. If they arrive by ambulance, even before they are lifted out, a staff member goes to say, 'You're welcome here.' And truly they are."

"I suppose," I said, "some of them are afraid of not being welcome anywhere."

"Yes; in addition to the fear of pain, of abandonment, there's often the fear of being an insupportable burden to others. We do our best to ease that fear straight away. Basically, our objective is to help the very ill patient do what all of us should be doing all the time—living as fully and normally as possible."

"Isn't that difficult," I asked, "when someone is in pain or is almost incapacitated?"

"We tell our patients not to worry too much about physical pain because we can use a variety of pain relievers that eliminate it altogether, or at least contain it within bearable limits. As for being incapacitated, a person can be completely helpless and yet be made to feel important. We assure our patients that we need them, because we do. They are constantly teaching us things about their condition that we, as teachers, can pass along."

I remarked that most of the patients I had seen were in wards rather than private rooms.

"In wards," said the doctor, "people can have a sense of being needed because they help one another. It's part of our attempt to remove the isolation that too often surrounds the dying. Suffering of any kind is intensified by isolation."

The Hospice owes its origins to just such an experience in 1948, when a young Polish immigrant with no friends or family lay dying in a big London hospital. He talked of his sense of isolation and despair with a young social worker. She, in turn, told him of a dream she had of a Home where persons like himself could find privacy, dignity, and relief from pain during their last weeks on earth.

When he died, the young Pole left five hundred pounds to the social worker "to be a window in your Home." She went on to study medicine, but she never relinquished the dream. In 1959, planning began. In 1965, construction was started. The site, the seventy-bed building and the equipment eventually cost about half a million pounds, all of which was donated.

I asked the director if the Hospice was also a religious foundation.

"Yes," she said, "but we accept patients of any faith or no faith. We try to help each one in terms of his own beliefs or nonbeliefs. I do agree, though, with the Catholic sisters in a hospital where I once worked. They always said that faith makes all pain relievers work better."

"Faith in some sort of life after death?"

"I would say, rather, faith in life and death. Trust and faith in life and in death are not so very different. The willingness to say *yes* to death is an affirmation of life, I think."

"In these surroundings," I said, "do patients who have been atheists or agnostics sometimes turn to religion at the end?"

"Yes," the doctor said, "quite often the spirit seems to grow stronger as the body grows weaker. I like to think that it's not merely an escape from fear so much as the discovery of One who has been seeking them in different ways all their lives. In any case, when faith comes, it's able to give death a positive value, for the patient can then see it as an offering of all he has to God."

I spoke of the humor and gaiety I had encountered in the wards, and the doctor smiled. "Everyone is astonished by that, but there really is a lighthearted side to life here, you know. If the path towards death is a shared one, it needn't be desperate or even too solemn—so we have parties and laughter. Distractions and pleasures give temporary forgetfulness from pain or unhappiness. But there's also a deeper kind of joy that comes when a patient is able to make his way along the path that leads from the wistful or resentful 'I don't want to die,' to the quiet acceptance that says, 'I only want what is right.' "

I said slowly, "It is the absence of fear that impresses me most about your Hospice. How do you account for that?"

"One reason," the doctor said, "maybe that we try very hard to keep human needs and medical needs in balance, and supply both. In some busy hospitals, human needs are sometimes neglected in the medical battle against death. Here we think a cup of tea given slowly on your last afternoon is far better than infusions or tubes in all directions.

"Another reason for the absence of fear is that, contrary to popular belief, death isn't frightening when it's near, or when people are allowed to approach it in their own way. Resentment or acute anxiety at the end are so rare as to be almost nonexistent. What was it Pope John said? 'My bags are packed, and I can leave with a tranquil heart at any moment.' In a way, that's what we try to do here: help people pack their bags with what matters to them, with what they need."

"What would you say is the most important item?"

"The conviction that they're not going to die in meaninglessness. It's the feeling that enabled one woman to say to me, 'Tell my family that it was all *all right.'* Of course, no one can simply hand this serenity to patients. You just have to help them work through to it themselves."

I remarked that I had seen many visitors, including children. The medical director nodded. "Visiting is terribly important," she said. "It makes a patient feel that he's still a part of things, that people still care. We have no formal visiting hours here; anyone can come at any reasonable time. We have special rooms where patients can entertain guests. We particularly like to have children because we consider ourselves a community, and most communities have children running about. Also, they're a reminder that life is an ongoing thing."

"Do any of your patients ever go home?"

"Oh, yes. Some are able to go home for weeks, or months. In fact, about half of all our patients are in their own homes. Home care can be absolutely right or absolutely wrong, depending on circumstances. Without proper medical supervision and support, it can be disastrous. I remember one case where our clinic staff was asked to visit a young woman whose pain had become uncontrollable. Both she and her family had become so desperate that they had considered ending it all.

"We were not told about this until she died a year later. Instead, she spent most of that year at home as an outpatient, free from pain and able to enjoy life, to cook, even to shop for her family and care for her three children. She finally came in peacefully to the Hospice for her last few weeks. One of the things she said at that stage was, 'The children are a year older.'

"We know that this family has really begun to live once more, because the husband keeps in touch with us. You can imagine how different it would have been if they remembered only the misery and guilt of doing something desperate."

I asked this most unusual woman, "What advice would you give to people who have a loved one gravely or terminally ill?"

"I'd say: 'Try not to be afraid of death, or if you are, try not to let your fears dominate the situation. Don't let such fears make you turn away from the ill person, or baby them, or treat them with exaggerated caution in the name of sparing them.' The dying almost invariably have more courage and common sense than they're given credit for. Most of them can face up to adversity magnificently."

"Anything else?"

"Yes, I'd tell the family to keep in close touch with their doctor and call on him when they need him. I'd urge them to share everyday life with the person who shortly is going to leave them, bring news of the household or the community, ask advice about things. I'd tell them not to worry about what to say or not say; love doesn't need words; a touch or a glance will do. I'd remind them that while final illness may seem like a calamity, perhaps only in calamity may the patient find the meaning of the whole of the rest of his life, only then have the time and the quiet to think about things that have been said to him all of his life but which he has been too busy or too preoccupied to accept.

"Finally, I'd tell them they will probably have to go through some hard moments in which there will be pain and fear and resentment, but that when these things are turned into acceptance, an almost luminous quality of joy comes through."

Leaving the Hospice, I passed the window that has a place of honor, the window donated by the dying young man so many years ago. I recalled the medical director's words when I thanked her for her time: "Perhaps to some extent we have been pioneers in this field of medicine, but we are not the only ones. More and more people are working on this. More and more hospitals are beginning to realize that death isn't just the surrender of life, but a positive act worth doing well, an act that people need help to accomplish."

Outside, the day was calm and bright. Across the street were some tennis courts with people playing. I hesitated, knowing that from the windows of the Hospice patients would be watching this manifestation of life and health, watching while with courage and dignity they played their own roles in the quietly splendid drama of death. As I stood there some words of Shelley came unbidden to my mind:

> Death is the veil which those who live call life.
> They sleep, and it is lifted.

Maybe so, I thought, *maybe so.* And I walked on, strangely heartened, through the tranquil afternoon.

Gone Home

All that night the silver hand of the moon had gently lifted the sea. Now, under the sunrise, the ocean was flooding the beaches, racing up the creeks and inlets, inundating the vast green-and-amber prairies of marsh grass. Down on the Georgia coast, these high tides in the fall of the year are known as marsh-hen tides, because only then can those wary shorebirds be flushed from their hiding places. On this bright October morning, with a warm sea wind out of the east, I had promised to take my friend Jim marsh-hen hunting.

"Be at the dock at seven," I had told him. "If the tide comes up enough, we'll give it a try."

A sentimental gesture, really. As children on this coastal island, Jim and I had been inseparable. Barefoot, sun-burned, shaggy-haired, we fished and swam, netted shrimp, hunted for turtle eggs, caught and sold crabs, while the summer days slid by like beads on a golden chain. Then came different schools, jobs in different places, and years of separation, until suddenly, one day, Jim was back. Health problems had made it necessary for him to slow down, find a less demanding job. Besides, he said, he had never really been happy away from salt water.

Once or twice a year I would ask him to go out with me in my little outboard skiff. We would surf-fish or follow the winding creeks or walk the windswept beaches. When we did, it was as if time reversed itself and we were children again, with the old closeness, the easy humor and the complete acceptance instantly there. It can be this way, sometimes, when the shared experiences of childhood go deep enough.

This morning, though, as I drove down to the dock, a faint, unaccountable uneasiness rode with me. I told myself that it was probably a guilty conscience: I really had no right to be chasing marsh hens when there were a dozen more important things clamoring to be done. But I reminded myself that we would be back by midmorning. Besides, I had promised Jim.

He was there ahead of me, talking with Andrew, the old black dock attendant, who is over eighty but can still handle a cast net better than any other man I know. Jim smiled as I came up, his frayed fishing cap pushed back on his head, and the thought came to me that the years can change many things about a man, but not his smile or his eyes. He nodded at the light shotgun I was carrying, almost a toy. "Only one gun today?"

I had a reason for wanting Jim to do all the shooting. For the boat handler, marsh-hen hunting is a strenuous business. It's illegal to run the engine. You have to push, pole, or paddle the boat, sometimes against wind and tide, often through unyielding grasses. I didn't think Jim was up to that kind of exertion. A strange reversal of roles, really. In our Tom Sawyer-Huck Finn days, there had been times when Jim, older and stronger, had had to take care of me.

Andrew steadied the skiff as we climbed in. The area I wanted to hunt was five or six miles away, far down the lonely barrier beaches. Here, along certain creek beds, the marsh grass grew tall, and here we would find the birds. At full throttle, we could make the run in fifteen minutes —perhaps less, if the tide was high enough for us to cut across the marshes.

Jim sat facing forward, shoulders hunched a little, and I

knew that each landmark flashing past held the same memories for him as for me: the point where we beached the great hammerhead shark, the bluff where we found the Indian skeleton, the pine tree where the ospreys had a nest. It was like looking through an inverted telescope, everything clear and tiny and faraway. Now we ourselves were middle-aged, and different. But the shifting patterns of sea and sky had not changed, nor the rhythm of the tides, nor the ringing silences, nor the proud, aloof remoteness of it all. And for this we were grateful.

We came at last to the green aisles of grass that we were seeking. The long-billed birds flew. The little gun barked, the sound flat and small under the immensity of sky. He shot well that morning, my friend Jim. Even after the lapse of so many years, there were few misses. After each shot, he urged me to take a turn. Each time I put him off. I could hunt anytime, I said.

The sun grew hot; managing the boat was heart-pounding work. Several times, just for the salt-clean coolness of it, I went overboard to retrieve a bird. Finally, dripping and panting, I stopped to rest. The tide was ebbing, now; the green prairies were reappearing; it was time to go. Somewhere high above us a gull cried its creaking cry, and I remembered how we used to summon each other as children by whistling two bobwhite notes reversed.

"We've had a good day," I said.

He smiled and nodded. "One of the best."

"Ready to go?"

"Not quite," he said. "You haven't fired a single shot." He pointed to a wedge of marsh grass. "I think I saw a bird swimming there. Take the gun and let me paddle. I'll be unhappy if you don't."

I did not want any unhappiness to mar the morning. "Take it slow then," I said.

We crossed the shining interval of water. I leaned forward, gun ready, but nothing moved. "That bird must have kept going," I said. Then something made me turn around. *"Jim!"*

He had crumpled forward silently; his cap had fallen to the bottom of the boat. His right hand still clasped the weathered oar. I reached for his wrist. If there was a pulse, I could not feel it. In the sudden, enormous silence, time seemed to hesitate, stretch itself out of infinity, then rush back again. In that moment, everything was changed. And yet, strangely, I did not feel frantic or desperate or alone. It was as if the closeness we had felt was too strong to be canceled out so quickly, almost as if Jim were saying to me, "Yes, it's a heart attack; the risk was always there. But don't let this upset you. We came out together. We've had a magnificent day. We'll go back together."

I made myself unload the gun. I put a seat cushion gently under Jim's head. The engine caught on the second spin, and the skiff leaped forward like a released arrow—almost as if she knew. I steered with my left hand. With my right, I held Jim's wrist, still hoping for a flicker of pulse. I had to watch the channels, but now and then I glanced down. The color was fading from his face, but the sense of Jim's presence, of his personality, remained very strong.

The skiff trembled with the full thrust of the engine. The tranquil sun blazed down, and the startled herons flared up and away as I guided the boat around the great horseshoe bends, the hidden sandbars and the oyster-shell reefs. I knew, almost to the second, how long it would take to reach the dock—and a telephone.

Yet the queer dislocation of time—of past and present —seemed to persist. We were here in the hurtling skiff, but we were also carefree children, gliding home through this same October sunlight in an old rowboat with a bamboo mast and an oar for a rudder and a homemade sail. It was all one fabric, one seamless piece. Part of my mind still registered shock and disbelief. But another part, calm and accepting, had no regrets. This was the way Jim would have wanted it: no doctors, no hospitals, no fear, no pain—just one sudden, splendid step across the line.

With life and death placed so abruptly side by side, values shifted, and I seemed to see certain things sharp and plain: that we had been right, not wrong, to risk what we had been risking; that the true measure of life was not the acquisition of money or power or reputation—it was companionship and fulfillment and awareness; that intensity of awareness was the greatest of gifts—and that, therefore, no one should ever feel guilty for seeking out places or experiences where this awareness might be found. If anything, the guilt lay in not searching for them more eagerly and more often—for no one has unlimited time.

Ahead of me now the shore loomed close. I glanced down once more at the pale face beside me, and suddenly I was alone. The skiff drove on across the swirling tide, my hand still held his wrist, but Jim was gone. *Where?* I asked myself in a kind of sudden terror. *Gone where?* And heard no answer.

I cut the engine and flung a line to Andrew. He looked down into the boat and then at me, his old eyes patient and wise. He took off his hat with his free hand. "He's gone," he said, gravely and gently. "He's gone home."

I looked out across the water to the line where the marshes met the sky, and for the first time felt my throat tighten and something sting my eyes. "Yes," I said. "That's right. He's home."

Epilogue

There is not enough darkness in all the world to put out the light of one small candle . . . .

This inscription was found on a small, new gravestone after a devastating air raid on Britain in World War II. Some thought it must be a famous quotation, but it wasn't. The words were written by a lonely old lady whose pet had been killed by a Nazi bomb.

I have always remembered those words, not so much for their poetry and imagery as for the truth they contain. In moments of discouragement, defeat or even despair, there are always certain things to cling to. Little things, usually: remembered laughter, the face of a sleeping child, a tree in the wind—in fact, any reminder of something deeply felt or dearly loved.

No man is so poor as not to have many of these small candles. When they are lighted, darkness goes away . . . and a touch of wonder remains.